Table of content

Introduction

What's it like to rewire your brain? It is meaningless in one sense: this means the neuron-relate connections changes in your brain. All we know is preserved in the brain, and if it does not physically alter in some (usually routine) way, the brain cannot store information. The brain has been continuously rewired, even now. This meaningless impression is like saving a computer file. This switches hard drive status (bits turn on and off, etc.). Yet rewiring in a machine means opening up the sucker and changing the way that the system works. That is the non-trivial rewiring sense. You're your brain's developer. You could teach new skills to an old dog. The common theory until recently is that our minds were hardwired and unchangeable from birth. Nevertheless, the good news is that we continually change our minds from our daily experiences. While you assess your behaviors and care experiences, you can change how you think to behave and adhere. There is a variation in the brain between functional (constantly occurring) factors and structural factors. For instance, structural changes do not mean that you have invented a new piece of knowledge and information, but that you have changed the way you learn. We vary from one another in our ability to get things done, to understand, to think critically, to consider and gain new information. You do not have to know everything within hours, days and even months as you alter your beliefs, learn new things or become conscious of your repetitive responses to negative emotions. One approach alone isn't enough to effectively rewire the brain. The emphasis must always be on growth and success.

You need to tolerate different life experiences, pleasant as well as frustrating ones. For instance, some people are curious and not others. Your learning at college, school and work should not cease. Continuous learning is much more important than you believe in your success. The first way to boost your mind is by challenging everything. Instead of challenging it and being open to thinking, it is definitely much easier for information to be accepted. Addictions break people, ruin people's lives, destroy families. Whether it's overeating, drinking to excess, daily use of drugs or turning to sex or violence, it doesn't matter, we live within our brains, and we can be very subtle and expert at covering up things from ourselves. We may lie to oneself so well; we assume our own lies. We have very powerful circuits of gratification in our brains, important to our survival 100,000 years ago as a species. Sadly, those circuits can get tangled up in the world of today. Our contemporary world causes these strong and simple brain circuits to switch on very easily, and if we don't take care, we can get hyper-fed and want to make these brain chemicals "feel good" as high as before.

Fear is among the strongest emotion. This affects your body and mind quite intensely. Fear can create strong signs of reaction when we're in crises. Anxiety is a word we're using for certain kinds of fear that generally have to do with thinking of danger or anything going catastrophically wrong, not right now. Anxiety and fear can last and go for a short time, but they can last a lot longer, and you might get trapped with them. In some situations, they can control your life, disrupting your diet, sleep, thinking, commuting, loving life, or even leaving the house or going to work or school. This can prevent you by doing things you need or want to do, and also has an impact on your health. Many people get overcome by anxiety and want to deal with situations which might frighten them or make them nervous. Breaking this loop can be challenging, but there are many ways to do it. You will learn to feel less afraid and deal with anxiety, so you won't be hindered from living.

Neuroscience tries in terms of the molecules, membranes cells and cell sculptures that the brain, perhaps the world's most complex electrochemical machine, works in growth, plasticity, learning, memory, cognition and adherence. The human behavioral sciences, particularly psychology and clinical psychology, interact with human behavioral disorders and mentation. The way the brain is functioning in individual decision-making needs to be understood. Obviously, neuroscience's techniques make a better understanding of what people think or feel. Continue to use the Neuroscience methods to create a better human understanding.

Chapter 1: Human brain and its functions

The brain is a stunning three-pound organ that regulates all the body's functions, recognizes data from the outside world, and personifies the mind and soul's essence. Intelligence, imagination, feelings, and memory are just a few of the many things the brain governs. The brain is protected in the skull and consists of the cerebrum, cerebellum, and brainstem. Using our five senses, the brain gathers information: sight, smell touch, taste and hearing-often many at once. This assembles the signals in a way that makes sense to us and can preserve it in our mind. The brain controls our emotions, memory and speech arms and leg movements and the work of several organs within our bodies. With the advancement of functional and structural imaging, the brain circuits and regions related to anxiety disorders are starting to be understood.

Brain amygdala tends to be essential in modulating anxiety and fear. The amygdala and other limbic system components are linked to areas of the prefrontal cortex. Amygdala hyperresponsiveness may be related to reduced thresholds for activation when reacting to perceived social threat. When there is anxiety, certain brain regions, including the limbic portion of the amygdala, revitalize and start to release stress hormones. This interacts with the hypothalamus, warns the rest of the brain to the presence of a threat and activates a reaction to fight or flight. A panic disorder involves amygdala an area that makes emotional regulation and practicing easier but is not so critical to other anxiety disorders. Because of the links between panic disorder and interception, another part of the cortex, insula, is actually described as a likely perpetrator for panic disorder because interceptive perception is important.

1.1 Basic introduction to the human brain

The human brain is the center of command of the human nervous system. The brain is the most complex and massive organs in the human body. It consists of over 100 billion nerves, which interact in trillions of links called synapses. It receives feedback from the sensory organs and provides the muscles with information. The human brain has the same structure as any other mammal brain but is larger than any other brain in comparison to its body size. Some of its major functions include

- The management of blood pressure
- The production of hormones
- The production of sensory information.

Some facts about the human brain

- The brain is the largest of all vertebrates with regard to body size.
- It is 3.3 lbs. in weight. (1.5 kilograms).
- The male's average brain volume is 1.274 cubic cm.

- The female brain's average volume is about 1,131 cm3.
- The brain accounts for about 2% of a single person's body weight.
- The cerebrum is 85% of the brain's weight.
- It comprises about 86 trillion nerve cells (neurons) — the "grey matter" — and
- It also includes thousands of nerve fibers (axons and dendrites)—the "white matter."
- All such neurons are linked by dozens of connections or synapses.

Anatomy of the brain

Below is a summary of brain parts and how they relate to the activities and capabilities of the body.

The Cerebrum

The main part of the brain is the cerebrum. It is split into two parts, known as hemispheres. A groove called the interhemispheric fissure divides the two hemispheres. It is also known as the longitudinal fissure. Each cerebral hemisphere is divided into large regions, called lobes. Specific functions are correlated with each lobe.

Front lobes: The frontal lobes are the lobes which are the largest. They are situated in the front part of the brain, as suggested by their name. They organize activities of a high level, such as cognitive skills, problem-solving, reasoning, scheduling, and attention Emotions and impulse control are also controlled by the frontal lobes.

Parietals lobes: Behind the frontal lobes lie the parietal lobes. They function to coordinate and perceive sensory information from certain parts of the brain.

Temporal lobes: The temporal lobes are at the exact level as the ears on each side of the head. They manage specific features, like visual memory (such as facial recognition), verbal memory (such as language comprehension), and reading others' emotions and reactions.

Occipital Lobes: The occipital lobes are at the rear of the brain. They are heavily involved in reading and understanding printed words, along with other forms of vision.

The Cerebellum

The cerebellum is situated just below the occipital lobes, in the back of the brain. It involves fine motor skills, referring to the coordination of smaller or finer movements, particularly those incorporating the hands and feet. It also allows the body to retain its posture, balance and balance.

Diencephalon

The diencephalon lies at the core of the brain. This includes the:

- thalamus
- epithalamus
- hypothalamus

Limbic system

The limbic system is said to be the "emotional brain which comprises of four glands located within the cerebrum. The glands help in expressing emotions and controlling hormonal responses. These are:

Amygdala: Responsible for anxiety, memory and fear recognition the amygdala is found in the telencephalon (the highest-developed portion of the cerebrum). Inside the temporal lobe, it comprises of two almond-sized pieces of grey matter.

Hippocampus: The hippocampus assists with memory formation and cognitive development. It is there where short-term experiences are permanent ones. The centrally located gland is also what enables spatial awareness in humans.

Hypothalamus: The gland of the hypothalamus is related to circadian rhythm (sleep cycles), appetite, and some emotional responses. Hypothalamus is also responsible for controlling the pituitary gland and how hormones are produced.

Thalamus: The thalamus is essential for significant nervous and sensory processes, a crucial piece of grey matter that resides deep within the frontal lobe. All senses except for taste and smell, go through the thalamus to be processed into what is touch, sight and hearing.

Brain stem: The brain stem lies at the front of the cerebellum and is connected to the spinal cord. It is comprised of three main parts:

Midbrain: The midbrain helps to control the movement of eyes and process visual and audible data.

Pons: This is the bulk of the brain stem. It is situated beneath the midbrain. It is a network of nerves that help connect various parts of the brain. The pons also contains some of the cranial nerves starting out. Such nerves are active in the processing of sensory information and facial movements.

Medulla oblongata: The lowest part of the brain is the medulla oblongata. It serves as the heart and lung function control center. This helps to regulate other important functions, including respiration, sneezing and swallowing.

Left and right Brain

The brain's working areas or lobes are separated into right and left parts, too. The right side of the brain and the left side are responsible for multiple but unique roles. General dysfunction patterns can occur when the injury is on the right, left or diffused (scattered across both sides). Understanding the issues associated with these particular circumstances can help caregivers or health care providers understand an individual's needs better.

1.2 Brain's areas which influence anxiety

Anxiety is an entirely normal and natural aspect of being a human being. There will always be moments when we are more anxious or obsessed than others. Anxiety, though, is a much powerful, more frightening factor for someone that never goes away. Anxiety is a human's natural reaction that serves a purpose. The aim should not be to reject it completely — just to make it a balanced, sustainable part of the lives. Even if you don't have an anxiety-related illness, you still have had to live with it and work with it the only way you know. Anxiety is part of our world, just as pain, sadness and pleasure are, but the aim is to learn how to cope with it and how to stop it from becoming toxic.

Difference between anxiety and stress

Anxiety is a sense of fear and discomfort which alarm you. It's simply meant to put us in an enhanced sense of understanding, so we're trained for possible threats. Sadly, we are in danger when we start feeling extreme fear, or when we exist in a constant state of anxiety. Our bodies rarely shut off our reaction to fight or flight, and we cope on a day-to-day basis with the physical and emotional symptoms of fear, even when there is no trigger or purpose for them.

Anxiety may look like tension on the face, but the truth isn't that clear. Anxiety may be caused by stress, but stress may occur in other forms. Stressors can make a person unhappy, frustrated, worried or nervous, while anxiety is precisely the feeling of fear, despair and anticipation that we have described. You might never even understand what causes the anxiety or in some situations, without any clear "trigger" or purpose, it can occur on its own. Stress is often triggered by stimuli from outside, whereas fear is an emotional reaction. That's part of what actually makes fear special from pain, and also what renders it so difficult to maintain.

The anxiety-influencing areas of the brain are the following:

Amygdala. Memories of creepy incidents and other feelings and experiences are stored in the amygdala. The amygdala may be so reactive in individuals with anxiety disorders, that it overreacts in conditions that are not dangerous. Animal research suggests that for specific anxiety disorders, various parts of the amygdala are detected.

Hippocampus. Campus Another brain structure within the limbic system, the hippocampus, plays a central role in storing long-term memories and emotions. Research has found that in some women who have been abused as children, the hippocampus becomes smaller than normal, an occurrence that raises the risk for post-traumatic stress disorder and other anxiety disorders. Research shows that in some people with depression, the hippocampus becomes lower too. Stress plays a role in both anxiety and depression and can be a key factor here, as there is some evidence that stress in the hippocampus could suppress the production of new neurons (nerve cells).

Coeruleus locus. The locus coeruleus is a brainstem region that ultimately determines what brain signals deserve attention. In research with animals, the animals exhibited anxiety-like signs when the locus coeruleus was electronically activated. Some researchers believe that the same reaction can happen in humans.

Cortex Prefrontal. The prefrontal cortex is interested in decision-making, problem-solving and reasoning workouts. It also seems to have a hand in preserving experiences of extinguishing worries as might happen during therapy for an anxiety disorder and turning down the fear response. For example, one region of the prefrontal cortex helps control the response to stress by controlling the amygdala. Another field the ventromedial prefrontal cortex helps support the long-term loss of traumatic memories. Research indicates that the potential to do this may be influenced by the extent of the ventromedial prefrontal cortex.

1.3 what can happen to the brain while experiencing anxiety, worry, panic

Anxiety

From time to time, we're all getting anxious, but what occurs in the brain when this inevitable emotion casts a shadow? Anxiety is characterized as panic attacks, nervousness or fear of an occurrence or circumstance that could create an unfavorable result, such as an interview for a job or an examination. While some people may experience these feelings quickly subsiding, others may acquire anxiety disorders, where anxiety continues and worsens over time. Anxiety is a form in which the brain alerts us of danger. The release of hormones, including adrenaline and cortisol, is produced when the brain realizes that you are at risk. The hormones should go back to their normal levels once the crisis is over. Anxiety, though, will continually trigger you to feel threatened and contribute to an accumulation of these hormones. In fact, cortisol can influence everything from perception to decision making. While stress serves a purpose and can allow us to respond in risky situations, too much anxiety can have an unintended effect on our brain.

Seven effects of anxiety on your brain

1. This affects your short-term memory. When you feel forgotten during anxious times, there is a scientific explanation for that. the raised cortisol from chronic anxiety decreases the hippocampus, which is the "core of brain memory." The impact of anxiety on the hippocampus is well known, and constant anxiety can contribute to forgetfulness and confusion. It is worth noting that this typically occurs with chronic anxiety, not just periods of stress periodically.

2. It can make you more impulsive. People in a bout of anxiety can make snap decisions. This is because, in part, to the effect of cortisol on the prefrontal cortex. Cortisol repositions the prefrontal cortex, which is the part of our brain that helps us to make decisions. "This can result in impulsive behavior, poor decision-making and irritability. So next time you're feeling anxious, putting off making some big decisions could be a good idea.

3. It can lead to depression. Anxiety and depression are two disorders that often go hand in hand; however, they are different. "The anxiety can sometimes lead to depression symptoms. Depression can usually be caused by an anxiety disorder, and anxiety is normally a symptom of depression, according to the Mayo Clinic. If you're having trouble dealing with depression or anxiety symptoms, it may be time to seek professional help.

4. Your anxiety could be affected by how you were raised. There are many factors that influence whether a person suffers from anxiety, the environment and genetics. Several popular studies, including a study published in Child Development in 2018, indicate that the way you are raised can play a significant role in your anxiety.

Studies have shown that breastfeeding mothers have babies with even more cortisol receptors, which adhere to cortisol and dampen the response to stress," "Neglectful moms raised kids who became more prone to stress in life. These are called "genomic changes" because they impact the way genes are expressed while changing the actual genetic code. Such changes can also be passed on, ensuring. "the negative experiences of one person can impact future generations down the road."

5. It can cause insomnia. Nothing is worse than being nervous at night and finding it difficult to fall asleep. "Anxiety causes insomnia, as seen during the fight-or-flight response, by triggering the sympathetic nervous system. This affects our heart rate, breathing and brain waves which affect the quality and duration of sleep, Certain anxiety signs include feeling nervous, an increased heart rate, and rapid breathing, according to the Mayo Clinic. So, it's not just in your head— when you're battling anxiety, there's a scientific reason for sleepless nights.

6. It can impact your serotonin levels. Serotonin is one of the' feel-good' chemicals in the body," says psychotherapist Avery Neal, M.A., LPC, "It controls mood, anger, sex drive, hunger, metabolism, sleep, memory, the ability to interact and more." So, a serotonin-level deficiency could alter the mood. Our serotonin transporter gene deals with our environment, and due to this, some people are at higher risk for developed anxiety and depression.

7. This Impacts How Sensitive the Amygdala Is. Because your amygdala interacts with the rest of your brain to manage and store feelings, the amygdala may be extra sensitive for people with anxiety disorders. it overreacts to threats that aren't really dangerous, unintentionally activating the brain circuits that cause an emergency stress response." Therefore, in the long run, anxiety will be connected to those memories that are related to false hazards, and the brain will effectively make up its own fears.

Anxiety can have far-reaching, and sometimes surprising, effects on your brain, from releasing hormones to causing insomnia. If you are constantly feeling nervous, do not hesitate to contact a mental health professional.

Panic Attack

Feeling panic is a danger-friendly response. The subsequent rise in breathing rate and blood circulation offers the challenge for what is needed to fend off — or flee—. However, if there is no threat, feeling panic can be a major issue.

What happens when there is a panic attack?

While everyone can have a panic attack, panic disorder is indicative of the fear of having a panic attack. Heavy heart palpitations, difficulty in breathing, feeling lightheaded, and fear of having a heart attack, death, or going "crazy" are frequently recorded during an attack. Panic attacks usually peak in 10 minutes. It is not understood whether the physical symptoms cause fear or fear is what causes symptoms. Individuals with panic disorder often tend to have a higher baseline anxiety levels than those without the condition, which can make them more sensitive to internal body signs such as their heart rate and breathing changes— a mind-body relation sensitivity called interoception. This over-sensitivity could cause them to interpret an internal problem when there is none. Therefore, panic disorder may evolve without a specific cause, unlike phobias as well as other anxiety disorders whereby the source of fear is identified. In addition, unwanted panic attacks can turn into predicted panic attacks. For example, after a sudden panic attack on the subway, the subway can be the trigger for an anticipated panic attack.

What brain parts are associated with panic disorder?

Although the circuitry is poorly understood for panic disorder, scientists have a general understanding of what areas of the brain are involved. Deeper mechanisms involved in emotional and defensive responses— such as fighting or reaction to flight— appear to be playing a role in panic disorder. These include portions of the hypothalamus, and an area named the periaqueductal grey in the brain stem. Arousing these regions elicits signs of anxiety that are usually felt in panic disorder. Signals from such deeper brain regions are usually moderated by signals from the higher brain regions, as the ventromedial prefrontal cortex. However, in panic disorder, less activity may lead to an over-activation of such deeper brain regions in the higher cortical areas. The amygdala, an area that facilitates emotional regulation and learning but is not as critical for other anxiety disorders, is involved in a panic disorder. Because of the connections among panic disorder & interoception, another section of the cortex, the insula, has indeed been described as a possible panic disorder culprit as it is essential to interoceptive awareness.

Worry

Are you a worrier? Maybe unconsciously, you believe that if you're "worried enough," bad things can be prevented. The truth is, however, that worrying can manipulate the body so that it can surprise you. When worry is overwhelming, it can lead to the sentiment of great anxiety and even lead to physical illness.

Worrying is feeling uncomfortable or excessively preoccupied with a situation or problem. With extreme worry, the mind and body get into overdrive as you continually concentrate on "what could happen." In the context of excessive anxiety, you can suffer from high anxiety— even panic — during waking hours. Most chronic worries tell of having a feeling of hopelessness or false fears that raise their concerns. Ultra-sensitive to their surroundings and others' criticism, excessive worries can see anything— and anyone else— as a potential threat. Chronic worries can affect your everyday life so much that they can compete with your health, lifestyle habits, interactions, sleep and job performance. Most people who worry constantly are so nervous that they seek relief from unhealthy lifestyle habits like overeating, smoking cigarettes or using drugs and alcohol.

Excessive anxiety and worry cause a response to stress

Stress comes from every day's expectations and pressures. Examples of conditions that cause stress on a daily basis include long lines in the grocery store, peak hour traffic, a telephone ringing nonstop, or a chronic illness. When anxieties and worries get intense, you're likely to trigger the response to stress. The stress response has two components. The first is the challenge's interpretation. The second is an instant physiological response called the "fight or flight" response that sets your body on red alert. There was a time our ancestors were protected from dangers such as wild beasts that could feasibly make a meal out of them by the response to fights or the flight. Although we usually do not encounter wild animals today, there are still dangers. In the form of a challenging coworker, a colicky infant, or a fight with a loved one, they are there.

Can Extreme Worry Make a person Physically ill?

A number of health issues may emerge from persistent worry and mental stress. The problem arises in the day-to-day fight or flight due to excessive anxiety and worry. The fight or flight reaction triggers stress hormones like cortisol to be released by the sympathetic nervous system of the body. Such hormones can raise levels of blood sugar and triglycerides (blood fats) which the body can use for fuel. The hormones can cause physical reactions such as difficulty swallowing Dizziness Dry mouth Rapid pulse Fatigue Headaches Inability to focus Irritability Muscle cramps Muscle tension Nausea Physical energy Continuous breathing Shortness of breath Trembling and twitching When the excessive fuel in the blood is not used for physical activity, major depression and severe outpouring.

While the effects are a reaction to stress, stress seems to be the spur. Whether you get sick or not based on how you cope with the stress Physical reactions to stress include the immune system, the heart and blood vessels and how certain glands secrete hormones in your body. Such hormones help regulate different functions in your body, including brain function and nerve impulses. All these mechanisms communicate with each other and are strongly influenced by the coping style and psychological state. It's not the pain that makes you sick. Rather, it is the effect of reactions such as excessive worry and anxiety on these different interacting systems that can lead to physical illness. However, there are activities you can do to change the way you react, such as changes in lifestyle.

1.4 Different areas are responsible for different fears, threats

The term "fear" relates to human behavior characterized by a consciousness of fear, and it is therefore not obvious whether similar emotions also occur in other species. "Fear" is also used in the field of neuroscience to refer to the mutual defensive reactions elicited by hazards across species and also sometimes to the neural systems that arbitrate these responses. We prefer a more general definition of "fear" as a central state that is stimulated when the individual perceives danger and mediates physical and behavioral reactions to this threat. These responses include defense mechanisms necessary for the individual's survival and which can be witnessed in virtually all animal species. Fear responses are caused by a number of stimuli, including predators, hostile members of a certain species, pain, and hazardous environmental features such as heights. Importantly, these varieties of stimuli strongly and continually induce defensive behaviors and are not dependent on the observation of direct harm correlated with the threat, nor on a learning process imputing the threat a valence of risk.

Two pathways of fear

Work on rodents by the neuroscientist Joseph LeDoux has helped us understand the brain circuitry of fear There was both a "low road" and a "high road" of fear, LeDoux suggested. The "low road" included stimulation of the amygdala, a midbrain mechanism that helped to identify a danger to our safety and set a biobehavioral reaction in motion that would encourage battle or fleeing. This reaction includes rapid respiration, fast heart rate, trembling, and other bodily responses that we perceive as fear subjectively. This "emergency" fear response is very fast to optimize our survival. LeDoux further described a "high road" where knowledge migrated to the prefrontal cortex (the brain's CEO or executive working center) first where it was stored before being transferred to the amygdala. This path was slower, allowing time to examine the scenario in greater depth. In this case, the prefrontal cortex could "reign throughout" an overactive amygdala, resulting in a more modulated and complex reaction of fear to varying threat levels. The amygdala is hyper-responsive to danger in people with anxiety or stress symptoms (PTSD) while the prefrontal cortex is under-active and lacks sufficient neural connections to the amygdala to calm things down. The effect is an increased and/or expanded reaction to terror.

Fear versus worry

Brain researchers have recently found that fear and anxiety/worry may have different neural circuitry. Fear can be seen as the solution to imminent and present danger, while anxiety/worry implies a reaction to unknown and possibly negative future events. Although fear-arousal originates from the amygdala, anxiety tends to be correlated with an area of the brain known as the stria terminalis (BNST) known as the bed nucleus. THE BNST is a basal forebrain system with substantial integration to many other regions of the brain engaged in the transmission of bodily functions, danger reaction, memory, attachment and information. In situations of confusion where something negative might arise (e.g. waiting for the results of a medical test or a job interview) the BNST is more involved than the amygdala, while the amygdala is more successful in posing a danger.

Other brain areas involved in fear, anxiety and stress

The medial prefrontal cortex Tumisu/Pixabay Source: Tumisu/Pixabay Medial prefrontal cortex (MPFC) is a region of the prefrontal cortex implicated in the processing of information about us and others. PTSD case studies find that this category has less MPFC activity overall compared to healthy controls. However, in reaction to anxious expressions, individuals with PTSD do have more MPFC stimulation than controls. The similar is found in people with social anxieties–less threat activation and more social activation. Low activation in reaction to danger can be seen as a deficiency in controlling emotions while high activation may be an effort to overcompensate for unnecessary anxiety in the lower brain areas, although more work is needed to explain this.

Many researchers investigated the degree of interaction between MPFC and amygdala in people with anxiety and stress conditions and healthy controls. These studies in people with PTSD and social anxiety disorder found less connectivity between the amygdala and MPFC. This indicates that under these circumstances, the MPFC is less in a role to control nervous reaction.

The insula

The insula is a small part of the cortex, deep inside the brain's lateral sulcus and not noticeable from the surface. It has a variety of functions, like higher-level perception, reaction, and control of senses. For patients with a social anxiety disorder or PTSD, the insula has been shown to be overactive for a response to threats in fMRI research. For social anxiety disorder, this reduced through stimulation by both treatment and psychotherapy. Therefore, the insula tends to be an environment creating anxiety and threat reaction, and a possibly fruitful target when we are looking for new ways to minimize fear.

The anterior cingulate cortex

The anterior cingulate cortex (ACC) is found between the neocortex and the brain mental (amygdala, hippocampus) centers. The tasks are diverse but tend to include control of interpersonal events and socially driven experiences. When it comes to fear and anxiety, different parts of the ACC seem to have different functions. The ACC dorsal component (dACC) tends to be interested in magnifying our danger reaction and is hyperactivated in individuals with panic disorder, phobias, and PTSD. Cognitive-behavioral treatment in people with social anxiety has been shown to reduce dACC activation, perhaps by helping change the way we view ourselves as well as others in social circumstances (although this is speculative). On the other hand, the rostral portion of the ACC (rACC) tends to be active in controlling anxiety and the reaction to attack. Lowered activation in the rACC in reaction to danger (meaning: reduced control of fear response) is shown in individuals with social anxiety disorder, PTSD, and common anxiety disorder.

The hippocampus

The hippocampus, which is our verbal memory core, interacts directly with the amygdala and the prefrontal cortex. The hippocampus can thus enable us to dampen anxiety by creating memories that tend to calm us down or improve our trust in managing the situation. For example, we might remember that we did not die and feel better for a while when we last had a panic attack, or we might realize that we survived the ordeal and were no longer stuck in life-threatening situations. On the other side, when faced with similar circumstances, the hippocampus will raise our fear or concern by reminding us of such negative memories. For starters, we might recall getting snubbed or omitted at a prior meeting when we are about to speak to a different person at a group. The hippocampus is more stimulated relative to healthy controls in response to threats in individuals with depression, phobia and social anxiety disorder.

New research utilizing fMRI scans to analyze the brain in real-time has shown that anxiety and stress problems tend to be "whole brain" symptoms, rather than just one or two brain areas. Amygdala, insula and anterior dorsal cingulate are the brain regions active in the production of anxiety and danger responses. Those areas involved in modulating and altering the response to fear and threat include the medial prefrontal cortex, the anterior rostral cingulate and the hippocampus. New understanding of the basic fear brain circuitry can inspire new ways to treat anxiety and stress symptoms or at least help us to understand which treatments work and why.

Chapter 2: Neuroscience and human nature

Neuroscience is the study about human's nervous system, and it has a deep connection with human behavior and human nature. Research in neuroscience includes substances, cells and paths all the way through active human behavior. Neuroscience combines physics, chemistry, and genetics with anatomy, physiology, and behavior research covering human emotional and cognitive functions. The two areas that seem to be separate from neuroscience that focuses on the mental equivalent's physical properties and psychology that focuses on the emotional equivalent. Moreover, neuroscience has to play a psychological role. Psychology and neuroscience may, in fact, be preparatory in various ways, except for disciplines which are entirely unrelated. Together they can lead to the solution to cognitive and behavioral problems such as psychology, neurological production and plasticity. To know how often the brain works neurologically and using technologies, including brain scans, helps to identify links between brain and psychological conditions. Millions of people are affected by brain and nervous system disorders every year, including Alzheimer's, Parkinson's disease, stroke and traumatic brain injuries. Such illnesses and injuries underline the relevance of biological sources of our behavior. Neuroscience related to human behavior perception is widely important not only in commercial research but also in branding, product monitoring and consumer experience. In reality, getting a mobile Neuroscience helps us to consider the customer experience in-store. It's necessary to understand how the brain works when it comes to customer decision making. Neuromarketing methods help make more sense of what people are doing and what products and brands they actually believe. Using the Neuromarketing tool create a better understanding of humans. Many forms of anxiety disorder arise in adults, where neuroimaging contributes to changes in some brain structures, depending on chronic and recurrent trauma experience. fMRI results in Generalized Anxiety Disorder (GAD) showed that the ventrolateral prefrontal cortex had a high level of activity. Although there are tremendous gains in understanding neuroanatomy and neuroendocrinology, not all anxiety disorders will necessarily be handled. Nonetheless, the most up-to-date study has broadened the range of medicines available for specific conditions of anxiety. For example, in the case of panic disorders, benzodiazepines are recognized as being more effective than GAD.

As neuroimaging technology continues to develop, growing information about the neurobiology of anxiety will influence how we handle anxiety and other related disorders.

2.1 What is Neuroscience?

Neuroscience, which works closely with the other disciplines such as math, linguistics, engineering, chemistry, computer science, philosophy, psychology and medicine, is an interdisciplinary science. Cellular, physical, physiological, biological, cognitive, genetic and cellular and therapeutic dimensions of the nervous system are investigated by neuroscientists. Different areas focus on different issues but often intersect. People with medical conditions such as Alzheimer's disease, researchers may investigate brain functions. MRI scanners and 3-D computerized simulations are part of the equipment. Experiments can be rendered using samples of cells and tissues. The results could lead to new medications being developed. Many neuroscientists participate in inpatient treatment.

Understanding Neuroscience

Neuroscience is a complex, multi-disciplinary science field that investigates the function and structure of the brain of humans and the nervous system. Brain, molecular biology, physiology and anatomy, human behavior, and perception and other fields are the foundation of neuroscience research for providing information regarding brain function at historically not understood stages. Human beings have approximately 100 billion neurons, or we can say brain cells, each with approximately 1000 ties to other cells. One of the modern neurosciences' greatest challenges is to draw up all cell-to-cell communication networks— the mental structures which process all emotions, feelings and actions. The resulting image, growing up bit by bit, is recognized as "the connectome," which underlines all learning by the capacity of the brain to build new links and neuroplastic circuits. Neuroscience is the way for neuroscience to learn the physical, psychological and neurological problems like the role of the brain in our understanding of different pain forms or the actual cause of Parkinson's disease. Computer simulations, visualization and other methods give new insight into the physiology of the brain, the five million km of wiring and its links to the remainder of the mind and body to researchers and medical professionals.

History

Ancient Egyptians felt that perhaps the heart was a knowledge organ for people. So, they extracted and discarded the brain as they mummified dead people but kept the heart intact. The brain has become the center of attention in terms of function and intellect in 1700 BC. The Edwinsmith Surgical Papyrus explains the signs, treatment, and likely results of two people who suffered head injuries, in ancient Egyptian brain writings. This is the first record of physical health and function connecting to the brain. Alcmaeon, a Pythagorean student who had lived about 500 B.C., argues the brain is where the intellect is, expanding human intelligence to include modes of thought. Hippocrates propagated Alcmaeon's assertion several years later by saying that the "brain is the mental headquarters."

Many hundred years later (384-322 BC), the Greek philosopher, polymath Aristoteles, questioned his theory when he announced that the human brain is the body's blood-cooling system and the heart the intellectual place. He also argued that people act more humanely and efficiently than livestock, as our larger brains more easily cool our blood.

They were able to understand the brain and its interaction with human functions only with the advent of the microscope in 1590. The first contemporary researcher in Italy to provide relevant knowledge of brain physiology was the early Italian physicist, scientist and pathologist, Gamillo Golgi (1843-1926). Golgi was able to show how individual neurons looked utilizing silver chromate salt. Santiago Cajal (1852-34) hypothesized that neuron is the tiniest functional unit in the brain on a building of Golgi's work, a Spanish pathologist and neuroscientist. Golgi and Cajal received the Nobel Prize in Physiology & Medicine in 1906 for their pioneering research and findings.

Several scientists from the 19th century, including the German physiologist, anatomist and herpetologist Hohannes Peter Müller, German physicist and physiologist Hermann von Hemholtz and the German physicist Emil du Bois-Reymond, have greatly increased their knowledge of the brain function by demonstrating the electrical excitability of brain neurons. In fact, the electrical status of the neighbouring neurons was determined by electrically stimulated neurons.

During the findings of Müller, Hemholtz, and Wois-Reymond, the French surgeon and anatomist Pierre Paul Broca proposed that the brain has several separate areas each liable for different human roles when dealing with people suffering from brain damage.

Modern Neuroscience

After the 1950s, the biggest progress and developments in neuroscience happened. Further discoveries and developments in related fields such as electrical pathology, molecular biology and computational neuroscience have been the source of the advancements in neuroscience since 1950. The knowledge of the brain, the nervous system and psychology are also enhanced by new technologies. Neuroscientists can now research the formation, growth, functions and diseases of the nervous system much more successfully.

At the beginning of the 1980s, physicists, including Donoghue, an engineering and neuroscience professor at Brown University, created techniques to find out exactly where brain activity happens when a portion of a body travels (arm, leg, and finger). Their results led to brain electrodes being developed. Donoghue and colleagues used brain sensors in an observation made in 2004 to track brain responses inside someone who suffered a serious spinal cord injury which left him entirely paralyzed. If he thought about raising his arms or legs–while his body could not generate action-they could track brain signals, they could see brain activity.

Major Branches of Neuroscience

While neuroscientists typically investigate many areas of neuroscience concurrently, the following divisions of analysis and subject-matter are categorized into Neuroscience. Behavioral neuroscience–trying to understand the effect of the brain on behavior. Concentrate on biological, behavioral sources. Cellular neuroscience–concentrate on studying neurons that make up the brain and the nervous system's structure and physiological properties.

Affective Neuroscience - To examine how neurons function in relation to human feelings is using animal research and testing.

Cognitive Neuroscience – The research and examination of human cognitive function. Cognitive science, psychology, linguistics and neuroscience are all found in this area of neuroscience. Standard cognitive neuroscience constructs exist. These include computational / experimental / modeling.

Clinical Neuroscience – Studying nervous system disorders.

Computer neuroscience - Trying to figure out how knowledge is processed by the brain. Brain function analysis takes place using advanced computer modelling and mechanics, algebra and other computational techniques.

Developmental neuroscience – Analyses the development of the cellular, nervous system.

Cultural Neuroscience – Explores how values and cultural factors over time affect the brain & genes.

Molecular neuroscience — Tries to understand how the nervous system is influenced by individual molecules.

Neuro-engineering – Use the techniques and principles of engineering to strengthen neural systems' understanding, repair and development.

Neuro-informatics – Using, evaluate, or enhance the knowledge and treatment of neural & Neurologic disorders by data collected throughout the fields of neural science. The analysis, advanced modelling, and data simulation involve neuroinformatic.

Neuroimaging - is a branch that focuses solely on the brain in the field of medical imaging. Neuroimaging is used for the treatment of brain diseases, cognitive research and recognition of neural responses.

Neurolinguistics –aims to understand better the neural mechanisms which affect language acquisition, understanding and expression.

Neurophysiology –provides a better understanding of brain function interactions and impacts different body parts. Use physiological techniques like electrode stimulation to analyze and examine different functions of the nervous system.

Paleoneurology –using ancient fossil analyzes to study brain growth, creation and processes.

Social Neuroscience –efforts at explaining how attitudes and social interactions are related to biological systems.

Systems Neuroscience — Information flow in a CNS to fully understand the roles and mechanisms of the CNS is figured out. System neuroscience uses the data gathered and findings to describe behavioral processes more precisely.

The Latest in Neuroscience

Just as the devices are electrically cabled, so the brain is neutrally cabled. These links combine its different lobes and also connect sensory input as well as motor output to the message centers of the brain, allowing information to enter and retrieve. The major objective of the present research into neuroscience is to investigate how this circuitry functions and what occurs when it is impaired. New brain MRI technologies enable clinicians to see some more detailed images and not only assess when harm can occur but also how the damage impacts behavioral functions and cognitive activity in disorders such as M.S. and dementia, for example.

Neuroscience discoveries have evolved in the last half-century in rapidly growing research by leaps and bounds. Further work is needed, though, to understand the neurological origins of human behavior, perception and memory fully.

2.2 Relationship b/w human psychology and neuroscience

Historically, detailed knowledge of biology was required in order to research psychology on the scientific level. In addition, William James has offered a perspective on The Principles of Psychology, one of the most current volumes on how psychology and biology contribute to each other. In the 1700s behavioral psychology as a field started taking a complex form after theorists decided to take a serious look at what the mind-body question had been called. This is, how closely connected is the mind and body. The unresolved problem examines the relationship between consciousness and brain—one is a set of mental, other physical. Issues about the relationship between these two properties largely support the brain-body problem. It is important to know if psychological conditions are medically distinct even if one is the next subclass, whether physical environments have an impact on mental conditions or vice versa.

Then there are concerns regarding consciousness, the physical body and the intent-what are these concepts? How do the body and the brain respond to them? Or does the mind pertain to the bodies, or is it the body just a mental place? There is no clear answer to these concerns, and therefore the dilemma remains unanswered, but the connection between mind and matter is explored in schools of thought.

Materialism–The materialist perception is that brains are only physical conditions.

Dualism–The dualistic perspective is that they are both real and can be related to each other.

Idealism–The idealistic view argues that physical conditions are mental states of fact.

Reductionism can also solve the problem. Constituent reductionism means that the brain produces mental processes, so the mind is a part of the body instead of a separate entity. The consciousness is believed to be brain function alone in eliminative reductionism.

Many neuroscientists do not think the consciousness can be described by brain function alone, so they define this assumption as emergent. Emergence happens when a company shows certain resources or behavior only when it communicates as part of anything else.

For example, water only takes shape if an oxygen atom binds to two hydrogen atoms, which are not liquid by themselves. The neurons in the brain are not aware, but consciousness arises through neural network mechanisms (Ludden 2017).

To analyze the facts, various psychologists retain the modern perspective that the brain does. The cognitive scientist Marvin Minsky initially put forward this point of view and can be strongly supported by evidence (LeadershipU 2019). Brain damage, such as medications and injuries, may influence the mind. People who have no brain have neither signs of awareness nor those who have a straight line for an EEG, that suggests that perhaps the mind does not exist alone but is developed by the brain (Tryon 2014).

Neuroscience Helps Psychology

The two fields that seem to be different from neuroscience that focuses on the physical properties and psychology that focuses on the emotional equivalent. Neuroscience, though, has a psychological role to play. In fact, psychology & neuroscience can complement each other in a number of ways, apart from being totally unrelated disciplines. Together, both can help answer cognitive and behavioral questions, such as neuropsychopharmacology, neural development and plasticity. Knowing how often the brain works medically and using technologies including brain scans will help identify connections between psychological and brain conditions. Neuroscience has introduced new and sophisticated ways to evaluate behavioral behavior-based mechanisms that allow clinicians in turn to make informed decisions about psychiatric therapies and treatments.

In fact, the association between psychology and neuroscience to positive effects, neuroscience has led to some interesting findings in regard to the following conditions influencing mental health and behavior:

Parkinson' s disease

Parkinson's degenerative nervous system disease causes brain nerve cell impairments that regulate the activity, also impacting the capacity of an individual to focus on the matter. Neuroscience leads to a more comprehensive understanding of the trajectory of the disorder, including the creation of estimation models to guide people in the region of the brain's basal ganglia. Scientists may help build treatments tailored to neural degeneration trends, as the interactions vary in Parkinson's patients.

Alzheimer's disease

Alzheimer's is marked by memory decline that contributes to a loss in intellectual skills and can induce emotional and behavioral changes. Researchers have found that age-associated loss of memory can be reversible with a gene transfer strategy by applying neuroscience to animals.

Scientists have found, in monkey experiments, that neuron activity in an area of the brain is decreased with age and that regulation chemical that affects thought, and memory stop making. Through adding and reinjecting a nerve growth factor into the cells into the monkeys' brains, scientists have been able to restore cell numbering and functioning, offering invaluable information on the possibilities for curing ageing diseases of humans (National Institute on ageing 2019).

Huntington's disease

Huntington's disease is caused by faulty DNA-sequence, which produces toxic protein and damages patient's neurons, which is a neurological disease that causes involuntary movement and disabled intellect. There is no cure yet for Huntington's disease, but neuroscience helps to find a solution. Over recent years work has introduced a number of different types of gene editing therapy, but a new system was developed over 2018 that was more effective and secure than previous ones. The newly developed device has been able to cut down the DNA strand, deactivate the defective gene and avoid the harmful protein from being generated and provide valuable data in order to warn Huntington's potential for future diagnosis (Frontiers Science News 2018).

Schizophrenia

Schizophrenia. Schizophrenia includes many mild manifestations of delusions and paranoia, a mental condition characterized by an altered perception of reality. Through the way of neuroscientific studies, scientists have made strides in classifying and linking conditions to brain structures and roles in order to help establish or enhance therapeutic approaches (Strik et al. 2017). Neuroscience frequently helps to develop research in the sense of a deterioration of treatment development for schizophrenia. Scientists have now found out when and where alterations of dopamine occur in patients' brains. Understanding the involvement of neurotransmitter systems and brain regions can assist in identifying key neurobiological characteristics of schizophrenia, e.g. changes in dopamine neurochemistry.

Clinical depression

Clinical depression, marked by low mood, has been treated in a variety of neuroscience areas. Results show that certain types of treatment work better for people with relatively regular baseline activation of the sub genuine anterior cingulate Cortis (Sg.ACC) region of the brain, whereas some have worked best with abnormal Baseline activation (Roiser 2015). Studies have been using brain scans before treatment in identifying changes in people with depression. Evidence can be obtained and used from such trials to make medication options for people with clinical depression. Many people are better able to respond to psychological therapy; some, for example, to pharmacology.

Autism

Autism is defined by a wide range of conditions and difficulties in fields including social skills, actions and speech, both verbally and nonverbally. Neuroscience research provides important knowledge on when autism is treated and how, as well as a glimpse into the aspects of brain activity. Scientists have been able to recognize structural and behavioral variations between autism-borne brains and associated spectral disorders and find that, as people with autism attempt, for example, to interpret facial expressions, the amygdala region of the brain is underactive. Because more males are impacted by autism than women, scientists often investigate the impact of fetal testosterone levels, discovering that higher prenatal testosterone rates are associated with reduced social skills but greater attention to childhood information–indicators of autism that can assist early detection (Cambridge Neuroscience, Cambridge University 2019).

Anxiety

Anxiety disorders are defined by a constant sense of discomfort or fear. Anxiety treatment with varying degrees of success can come in the form of therapy and/or medications. Nonetheless, after experts have established a brain mechanism, a recent discovery focused on neurosciences could improve how antianxiety medications are developed, which could be a new goal for anxiety-cutting medicines.

In the brain chemical transmission system called NPY, researchers have identified the mechanism that reverses the stress reactions caused by the hormone CRH in the brain-sensitive area of the amygdala brain. All chemicals use same pathways, and scientists have been able to detect and prevent anxiety-causing protein production, before finally, the channels vanish, thus providing a future target for the new production of drugs (University of Alberta 2018).

Drug abuse

Drug abuse is defined as unhealthy habits of consumption of alcohol or drugs that cause damage to the functioning of an individual. In recent years great research has taken place into the effects of drug abuse, including neuroscientific evaluations, that analyze how external influences affect unconscious treatment and lead to addiction. Various factors contribute to the initiation of dependency, and some neuroscientists believe that the economic status of an individual affects their wellbeing as well as the neurological basis of dependence, by involuntary care, thus creating a high need for external brain incentives (Farisco et al. 2018). These are only a few domains directly linked to psychology, where neuroscience makes a real difference–

neuroscience influences study and academic thinking in a wide range of different disciplines in numerous other ways.

Neuroscience explains Human Experience

The universe around them had always been highly sought by human beings. This was, without a doubt, part of the original purpose (though not the only one) Forces were the source of events of non-theistic societies–illnesses were triggered because' evil spirits' were attracted to the human body, and atmospheric patterns were induced by the wind and the storm. Gods (in the singular or plural) have been involved in theistic civilizations. Even if they did not cause things directly to the universe, the inhabitants got sick, experienced injuries, perished because it was God's intention. They now realize much more rationally how the world functions, which might be one explanation that faith no longer has such a key role in our society. Nevertheless, it is clear to see the same desire towards certitude even in modern science, to understand the necessary' explanatory content,' and to build connections when no one is there. The need to create an "explaining system," that often inflates and distorts proof, is quasi-religion.

The main explaining tool was genes until recently. Throughout 2000, geneticists traced the' human genome' in the expectation of discovering the genes responsible for all the human experience. It was anticipated that this would contribute to a change in our understanding of everything from the cancer to human consciousness. (A genome was sometimes referred to as' the book of life') These were the' genes' years when a scientific basis for all was supposed to exist. Genesis made people human, violent, sexual, hormonal, alcoholic, intellectual, and suicidal (or at least hereditary processes.

But the search for the genome was a deception. This raised more questions than answers and showed that genes are far less important than anticipated. It found that people have only approximately 23,000 genes, much less than assumed— just half as many as tomatoes. The genetic map shows little difference between humans and other animals (for example, chimpanzees). Surprisingly we have also observed that inherited traits, including height, contribute only to genes quite marginally. After all, there are no "genes around." However, more common diseases tend to have no hereditary origin, so as others conclude, the initiative has not provided significant medical results. "Faulty genes never trigger or even slightly predispose us to, illness and therefore the study of human genetics is in deep crisis," says Jonathan Latham, director of the Bioscience Resource initiative.

Neuroscience, an explanatory tool

The explanatory focus has now moved from the genome to the human brain. The new predictive fad is neuroscience. It's not more genes but "neuronal pathways" that are responsible for everything. Many neuroscientists have reported understanding the brain activity–or brain sections–correlated with fear, artistic thinking, artistic enjoyment, political affiliation (Republican neurology is distinct from democrats) and many more. And here, of course, there is often a causal connection. A certain type of neurological research is correlated with violence so that, in principle, attackers could be' healed' if these habits were reversed, perhaps through neurosurgery or medications. We have been influenced by the so-called neuromania of the psychologist Raymond Tallis.

2.3 relationship b/w behavior and brain

In late 20th century, methods were established for observation of the behavior of the living brain which enabled us to explore relations between what brain has been doing and psychological phenomena. The brain works helps you to do, experience, and learn everything you do. (FMRI) Functional magnetic resonance imaging is used to analyze brain activity and track blood flow variations by analyzing the magnetic fields produced by active nerve cells in the brain. Consumers can use computation to convert such material into pictures that literally "illuminate" because they conduct mentally different perceptions, photos, feelings, and emotions in different fields of the brain. This makes it possible to examine much more accurately and in-depth the relations between brain activity and the subconscious when reacting to various stimuli and producing specific emotions and thoughts. These can vary from feelings and photographs, for example, to those who are more willing to hate and terror. Such a technique has culminated in a technological learning movement using the cellular stage of neural activity to discuss issues that are of central concern to psychologists employed in almost all specialty fields.

Brain-Behavior Relation

The relation among brain and behavior seems to be the heir of this renowned Cartesian dualist mind-body in which the brain is the physical or biological part. The body-mind dichotomy appears to be an unsolved issue, given its ancient origins. All definitions were held as if they were distinct and separate. But the idea of the separate function of mind and body is an obstacle to scientific progress because mind and body are more complexly linked than one would imagine. Most people will answer "to understand, interpret, reason, or know." Although it is accurate that the brain does such things, they also serve as the basis for the ultimate goal–to lead. We will know what's happening in our surroundings, for example, from our awareness, causing more efficient and proactive behavior.

The goal is, therefore, to connect all brain activities to certain behaviors. But it's not all that easy. For example, various physiological pathways can activate the same behavior: we may drink a beer as we are thirsty or because we feel anxious and want to use its poisonous impact. First of all, if we had the brain of a scientist, we would be the genius, as we think the brain takes blame for our actions. Yet this is becoming more and more difficult. We shouldn't underestimate the capacity and strength of the brain. The organ grows and evolves to the changing climate during life. Therefore, the brain-behavior interaction is modified by different factors: the climate, our personality, and our cognition and behavior. The atmosphere modulates the creation of various skills, for instance. For a child who comes from an urban area in rural areas, language acquisitions can, therefore, vary (because verbal reinforcement is specific for each infant).

The enriched environment is another case. It has been shown statistically that people living in enriched environments have better synaptic connections between neurons (because an enriched environment allows individuals to respond and enhances cognitive & sensory stimulation) than in bad environments. Of comparison, the production of the nervous system can have environmental factors. An example of this is early life malnutrition. It is therefore shown that the environment can change our brain and thus influence future behaviors.

Social and historical aspects: our attitudes would have been very distinct from those of the geniuses at the moment if we refer to the illustration. The socio-cultural and historical background would have quickly been modified, unquestionably distinct from Einstein and Mozart.

Phylogeny: a human brain with a background of phylogenetics, i.e., heritable evolutionary traits. The brain can, therefore, discern between three different layers: core or reptilian, an intermediary or limbic layer (the earliest phylogenetic layer), and outer or neocortex, which differentiates humans from other species. So, the brain undertakes modifications when we mature into a species in order to satisfy the specific environmental requirements.

Genetics: gene expression regulates the creation of our brain. To a degree, it can cause variability, such as specific incentive sensitivities, various likelihoods of behavior. On the other side, the mechanism differs and can cause different diseases if a mutation occurs in the DNA.

Ontogeny: meaning the individual's growth and what we've experienced in a lifetime. The present conduct relies on past experiences. These have been contained in our memory as well as serve as a guide to some and no other behaviors. Another reason is that we tend to repeat it if we have found enjoyment inactivity in the past. The changes in behavior reported after a brain injury often reinforce the mind-behavior relationship; nonetheless, neuroscience attempts to relate various brain structures and actions, mainly through the study of brain lesions. Neuroimaging methods are therefore used to assess a lesion location and to analyze the person's neuropsychological history. If the trend is replicated in many cases, the affected condition can include a certain brain region.

All this demonstrates that the interaction between the brain & behavior is dynamic and interdependent. The brain gathers information and internal & external influences that make the best behavior. The actions also have environmental effects that can be positive or negative for all of us. Such results allow us to understand and reduce the chances that this will happen again in future. This results in brain changes, particularly synaptic interactions between the cortex and the hippocampus.

2.4 Use of neuroscience to better understand human behavior

The launch of brand techniques and new products requires a profound understanding of the needs and desires of people. Marketing experts have historically depended upon people to ask questions in order to collect such knowledge. It assumed that people knew what they really needed. We started watching people in their houses and during shopping as we applied sociology to our toolkit. Their interests became better known, and their unmet needs started to be expected.

Technology-enabled us to better analyze the data and predict the outcome based on past behavior. This enhances the understanding of behavior. These instruments enable us to provide a better history of human behavior. We found, though, that citizens could not properly articulate what they actually thought or wanted. It is because in our unconscious so much is contributing to what we do and do. Industries have started to incorporate scientifically new tools such as implicit analysis techniques to assess the latent correlations people have in relation to ads, labels, goods and packaging. Implicit reaction primes the subjects with the photos and categorizes them into words no.1 Neuromarketers are willing, without posing specific questions, to identify and quantify the immediate response.

At least three separate groups can be listed as the Neuromarketing Toolbox.

- Behavioral measures: visual coding may be used to analyze the behavior of customers in order to determine an emotional response or specific mental states.
- Psychological measures: body measurements from the twitch of the head, dilatation of the eyes, rubbing of the hands, pacing and rhythms. Such tests are associated because of the wired existence of the brains and the central nervous system.
- Neuroimaging: the most commonly employed neuroimaging techniques are functional magnetic resonance imaging (fMRI) and electroencephalography (EEG). EEG and Eye Tracking are most often used together because they calculate what people have noticed and are interested in what they have observed.

Neuromarketing is among the top 40, according to the most recent Green Book Publication, the most popular research suppliers. Unconscious behavior analysis approaches are becoming simpler and more available. Ten years ago, the start and operation of new Neurolab cost millions and a laboratory can now be set up for a percentage of this cost.

Neuroscience is very applicable not only in ad testing, as well as in brand positioning, consumer experience and package testing. Yes, Neuroscience mobile helps us to understand the experience of our clients in the store.

Knowing how the brain works are critical in the decision-making process of consumers. Neuromarketing methods help make clearer sense of what people want and care of brands and products. Let us start using our Neuromarketing instruments and build a better understanding of humans.

2.5 The anxious mind- Neuroscience of anxiety

Individuals with an anxiety disorder undergo attitude and body function changes based on neurology, which are addressed in greater detail in this post. As with terror, the relationship between the genetic coding & environmental factors results in different temperament and emotional responses. Our genes are more responsive to certain particular triggers and contribute to the development of resistance to other stimuli. A plastic structure is our brain. The role of external factors cannot, therefore, be denied in their development and casting.

Fear and stress are natural protective reactions to threats which help our bodies cope more effectively with challenges. Anxiety varies from anxiety because it is a series of mental and somatic responses to a potential or unlikely future threat. Anxiety is a regular human response to some degree. It can, though, have a negative impact on our everyday living and wellbeing if it lasts for a long time. Concerning the future, it is difficult to concentrate on the circumstance of fear which contributes to irritability. Also, in this condition, somatic symptoms such as palpation, sweat, and gastrointestinal changes. If such signs occur for six or more months, fear is deemed a disease. Discussions of anxiety are most common among people with psychiatric disorders and involve around 10% of the population at any time. Nonetheless, only a few of those with anxiety disorders are seeking treatment. The challenges with defining the disorder will partially explain this. Some of the most common forms of anxiety disorders are generalized anxiety, panic disorder, acute phobia and social anxiety.

What makes an individual susceptible to anxiety conditions?

Including clinical as well as observational studies have shown the legacy of different forms of anxiety disorders. A variety of twin studies have shown the importance of family clustering in anxiety. Other inner factors, such as certain characteristics, make that person more vulnerable to anxiety.

Including internal factors, environmental factors might also raise the anxiety of certain individuals. Exposition to stressful conditions, drug or alcohol use, family-style and stressful life events include these factors.

Stress and anxiety neuroanatomy. In the prefrontal cortex are higher cognitive centers within our brain. We are concerned with social interaction, learning and preparation. The "newer" part of the brain from an evolutionary point of view helps us keep our emotional reactions in check. Within ancient areas of the brain, most of the mental therapy takes place. Such functional brain structures are recognized as the "limbic system." The hippocampus plays a significant role in response to stress and control of the hypothalamic-pituitary-adrenal (HPA) axis is a central part of the limbic system. The development of stress resilience and anxiety is based on both hippocampal growth and neurogenesis. Yet amygdala may be the essential part of the limbic system, which plays a key role in emotion regulation. Amygdala has proven hyperactive in anxiety disorders and is central to the development of terror and distress memory. It is well connected to other components of the brain such as the amygdala, Thalamus and Hypothalamus. In addition to structural adjustments, it is important to understand that neurotransmitters can provide brain connectivity or contact between different brain centers and networks. Gamma-aminobutyric acid (GABA), known to inhibit the emotions, has an excitatory effect in the case of emotional response. Also well established in the pathogenesis of different emotional states are the functions of serotonin, dopamine and norepinephrine. Cholecystokinin (CCK), galanin (Gal), neuropeptide Y (NPY), oxytocin (O.T.), vasopressin (AVP), and corticotransmitter can also enact in the pathogenesis of anxiety disorders. Component of corticopressine secretion.

Neuroanatomical alterations in stress. The majority of cases of anxiety disorder occur in adolescents, where neuroimaging results in improvements in certain brain structures, based on prolonged and repeated history with anxiety. FMRI findings of Generalized Anxiety Disorder (GAD) found that the ventrolateral prefrontal cortex had a strong level of activity. In fact, there is a substantial activity level in the amygdala, especially when people are asked to focus on their tension and adjustments in their cingular and insular cortex.

The physical development, as well as changes in behavior, intellect and emotional control, become increased throughout puberty. During this time, regeneration of the body will lead to permanent improvements in different brain regions that can be involved in the development of adult psychiatric disorders. Using cognitive therapy or other approaches, it may be simpler to restructure multiple brain structures through puberty than in adulthood. Meanwhile, different treatment agents can be used in adults to alter the brain's biochemical structure. The first phase of therapy is often recommended for people who have anxiety disorders, specific serotonin reuptake inhibitors (SSRIs) and serotonin-norepinephrine reuptake inhibitors (SNRIs). The monoamine oxidase inhibitors, tricyctic antidepressants and benzodiazepines are other drugs that can be used for the diagnosis of different anxiety disorders.

Although we have made tremendous strides towards learning neuroanatomy and neuroendocrinology, it is not actually possible to treat all anxiety disorders. Nonetheless, the most up to date study has expanded the range of medications accessible for specific anxiety conditions. In the case of panic disorders, for example, benzodiazepines are recognized to be more efficient than GAD. Increasing information about the neurobiology of anxiety will affect how we handle anxiety as well as other related disorders as neuroimaging technology continues to develop.

Chapter 3: Addictions and their effects on the human mind

There are different addictions, and each addiction has a different impact and effect on the human mind/brain, health and behavior. A person who is an addict consumes or performs a substance which provides an opportunity, given adverse consequences, to replicate the behavior. Persons with GAD are much more likely than people who do not have the anxiety to become addicted to drugs as well as alcohol. When disorder effects intensify, individuals may switch to drugs to cure themselves. Drugs and alcohol are used as a means of escaping reality, relieving the signs of anxiety, and creating a sense of satisfaction. A limbic system is the brain part with its center of pleasure. The potential to experience pleasure is controlled and regulated. We end up repeating them when practices are enjoyable. The healthy and positive activities such as food, exercise and time with friends and family and friends stimulate this system. Drug use and alcohol have an enormous brain effect. That's the body part that regulates important vital functions such as breathing. It also enables you to interpret all of your sensory impressions and your emotions and feelings. All of these factors affect your behavior. Treatment is required to break the cycle of addiction. In fact, addiction is hard to treat as a chronic disease that requires constant care. It does not work by only telling a person to abandon, and there is no solution to addiction. Fortunately, however, addiction has also been dealt successfully.

3.1 The brain and different addictions – GAD

The word "addiction" originated from a Latin term for "enslaved by" or "bound to." Everyone who has tried to overcome an addiction— or tried to help someone else do so understands why. Addiction exerts a long and strong impact on the brain, which occurs in three distinct ways: compulsion for the source of addiction, lack of control over its use and alleged involvement with it despite harmful effects. While it is possible to overcome addiction, the process is often long, painful and difficult. Today we understand addiction as a chronic disease that affects both the structure of the brain and its functionality. Just as the cardiovascular disease affects the heart and pancreas is weakened by diabetes, so does alcohol hijack the brain. Addiction treatment requires willpower, obviously, but "just say no" is not enough. Rather, people usually use multiple methods— such as psychotherapy, medication, and self-care— as they attempt to break the grasp of an addiction.

There has also been an important change in the thought around addiction. Researchers claimed that addiction could only be caused by alcohol and powerful drugs for many years. However, neuroimaging techniques and more recent research have shown that certain pleasurable behaviors, such as gambling, shopping, and sex, can co-opt the brain too. An edition of the Diagnostic and Statistical Manual of Mental Disorders (DSM-IV) identifies multiple addictions, each connected to a particular substance or behavior, there is consensus that these can reflect multiple manifestations of a similar underlying brain process. Addiction affects multiple levels of the brain. Stimulants, caffeine, morphine, alcohols and sedatives include chemical compounds that penetrate the brain and bloodstream after each use. Once a chemical gets into the brain, they may lose control and desire for a toxic substance. The brain wants the pleasure of the drug when a person develops an addiction. This is because the brain's reward system has been stimulated intensely. Most people use the drug to activate many euphoric feelings and unusual behavioral traits in response. Long-term addiction may result in severe effects, such as damage to the brain, and can even lead to death.

Substance-related addictions

It involves obsessive misuse of the following:

- Tobacco
- Alcohol
- prescription drugs
- Street drugs

Behavioral or process addictions

Although less well studied, several behaviors seem to perpetuate properties and may include excesses correlated with:

- Gambling
- Food
- Sex
- The Internet
- Video Games
- Work

From liking to wanting

No one begins to develop an addiction, but a lot of people get caught in the snare. More than two-thirds of addicted people are using alcohol abuse. Marijuana, opioid (narcotic) pain relievers, and cocaine are the top three drugs which cause addiction. The possibility of development of an addiction is affected by genetic susceptibility. Twin and adoption research show that the propensity to addiction is hereditary from about 40 to 60 per cent. Yet behavior, especially when it comes to improving a routine, plays a key role.

Principle of Pleasure. Whether the brain has psychoactive medication, a cash reward, sexual encounters or a pleasurable meal, it records all sensations the same way. Pleasure has a distinct hallmark in the brain: the production of the neurotransmitter dopamine in the nucleus accumbens, a network of nerve cells located under the cerebral cortex. Dopamine secretion is so strongly linked to enjoyment in the nucleus accumbens that neuroscientists point to the area as the source of pleasure for the brain. The addictive drug offers a gateway to the brain's compensation system by delivering dopamine into the amygdala. A quick feeling of pleasure is retrieved in the hippocampus and amygdala produces a programmed reaction to certain stimuli. All drugs, including tobacco to cocaine, have produced an especially high amount of dopamine in the nucleus. It is directly related to the speed of release of dopamine's, the frequency of release, and the durability of release, the probability that the use of or involvement in a satisfying behavior may contribute to addiction. Even the same medication will affect the risk of addiction through different management strategies. By comparison to consuming it as a tablet, for example, smoking or injecting a medication usually produces a better, higher dopamine sensation and is most likely to cause drug addiction.

What Increase risk factor for addiction

No one is doomed to become a lifetime addict from birth. Many genetic factors increase the probability of addiction but so do experiences that influence the development of the brain. Experiences that occur early in childhood can change brain structure in ways that make an individual almost likely to develop an addiction later in life, even as far back as the prenatal and postnatal periods. For example, the nature of the relationship between the infant-caregiver and the vulnerability to Toxic Stress both have immediate effects on the brain structures that control the emotions and stress. In other words, children exposed to toxic stress will grow into adults who find it difficult to cope with stress, anxiety and mood. This may lead people to try self-medication in an attempt to relieve these effects.

Becoming addicted is a gradual process including the interplay over time of genetic factors, early interactions and the impact on specific brain systems with potentially addictive drugs and experiences.

Reward and motivation

The brain reward circuit is activated by compounds and experiences with addictive potential. These stimuli are also called reinforcer because we are more likely to engage in them again due to the pleasurable sensation, we get from them. Both alcohol and illicit drugs, including food, sex and gambling, are strong reinforcers. These substances and experiences induce the release of large quantities of the neurotransmitter dopamine in the reward system of the brain. In these circuits increased dopamine levels over extended periods of time result within physiological and chemical changes as the brain tries to restore equilibrium. Such changes eventually underlie habits such as bingeing, worsening use and withdrawal symptoms after taking away the medications or interactions.

GAD - Generalized Anxiety Disorder and addiction

There are often linkages between mental health and substance abuse. When this occurs, the connection between the two can be quite complicated, with each getting multiple negative effects on the other. This is a co-occurring disorder or dual diagnosis when a substance use disorder occurs with a mental health disorder. According to the American Anxiety and Depression Association (ADAA), one such condition, generalized anxiety disorder (GAD), is extremely common in our nation impacting 6.8 million people, or 3.1 per cent of the population. Characterized by persistent and extreme worry, an individual with GAD can face long-term problems, including drug abuse and addiction, factors that only help to aggravate the anxiety.

Generalized Anxiety Disorder

Generalized anxiety disorder is a psychological disorder characterized by persistent and intense fear and anxiety to the extent that such emotions cannot be managed by a person. Such states of mind, approaching excessive levels, can exist for no clear reason, and may even emerge with the mere thought of meeting a single day. This persistent and often crippling illness will dramatically affect the quality of life of an individual by interfering with his daily activities and duties. Generalized anxiety symptoms go beyond the mental and include ways in which anxiety affects a person's physical state. There are several other factors in considering these elements which characterize the presence of GAD. According to the ADAA, as set out in the Fifth Edition of the Mental Disorders Diagnostic and Statistical Manual, a person must experience at least three of the following symptoms, for days usually spanning six months or more:

* becoming easily sleepy or lethargic
* Feeling nervous, restless or anxious
* Problems concentrating or keeping on to ideas
* Becoming irritable
* Muscle becomes tense
* Poor quality of sleep

Most of these things can cause adverse effects that trigger or aggravate anxiety. For example, a person unable to sleep or focus can fall back into their job duties; being nervous regarding job security, finances, etc. Such factors and consequences may be caused by even more troubled, dependent on abuse drugs, the use of substance disorders.

3.2 Addiction and its effects on the brain (Relationship with anxiety)

Anxiety is a feeling, expressed before an important event by a feeling of uneasiness, usually with unexpected results such as a job interview or a test Thus anxiety is the response of the body to stressful, risky, or unfamiliar circumstances. Anxiety is a healthy feeling at normal levels, as it helps us prepare for unknown situations by staying alert and conscious. However, people with an anxiety disorder encounter high levels of anxiety which can be daunting and life-threatening to the point of disrupting with the ability of the person to lead a normal working life. Anxiety disorders are a mental problem that keeps people from sleeping, from focusing on everyday activities, from socializing. This is because the person feels intense, irrational anxiety and excessive fear. As it leads to severe physical and psychological consequences, this condition can become uncontrollable.

Relationship between anxiety and addiction

It is common for people who have the anxiety to treat themselves or take alcohol or drugs to try to copy their symptoms. National Institute on Drug Abuse explains that anxious people are twice as likely to report drug and alcohol abuse as the general population. In addition, substance abuse is more common in anxiety disorder sufferers than in the general population. Anxiety disorders have been associated with higher lifetime alcohol abuse rates and higher relapse rates following drug recovery, according to Psychiatric Times. Furthermore, those infected with anxiety can suffer more serious symptoms of withdrawal. Misuse of alcohol or drugs enhances anxiety effects. The person gets trapped in a vicious circle: if they use more alcohol or drugs, they intensify the physical and psychological symptoms of anxiety, which helps them boost their consumption of medication to act properly. This contributes to the creation of drug tolerance and eventually to a process of substance abuse which leads to physical dependence and addiction.

Dual Diagnosis: Anxiety and Addiction

Dual Diagnosis: Anxiety and Addiction Double diagnosis (or co-occurring disorders) is the medical term defining the combination of a condition of an addictive illness such as depression, drug addiction or gambling with an anxiety disorder or other kinds of mental health issue. Several common factors for dual-diagnosis of anxiety and addiction, which induces anxiety to induce substance abuse or vice versa, are:

Self-medicating: anxiety-related people often use alcohol or drugs to regulate their physical or psychological symptoms. (e.g., a manager with a social anxiety disorder may use alcohol to interact with unpleasant presentations or business meetings)

Symptoms of substance abuse or withdrawal: alcohol and drug abuse also trigger anxiety-like symptoms (depression, sleeplessness, fear). Likewise, some common symptoms of withdrawal from alcohol or drugs include nausea, restlessness and sleep disorders.

Biochemical factors: Biological imbalances in the brain are related to both anxiety disorders and drug use disorder. For example, low levels of the serotonin neurotransmitter were correlated with both alcoholism and mental illness.

Genetic predisposition: Evidence exists that individuals who are prone to anxiety might also be prone to addiction if both conditions are present in the family history.

Addiction to drugs

People use addictive drugs to elevate moods, but repeatedly using these drugs lead to serious unwanted effects, including tolerance to certain drug-related effects, sensitization to others and the adaptive condition— dependence —

which paves the way for withdrawal symptoms once drugs usage stop. However, the most serious consequence of repetitive drug use is addiction: a constant state in which obsessive drug use evades control, even when severe negative effects follow. Addiction is marked by a long-lasting risk of complications often caused by drug-related exposure. Significant progress has been made in identifying the cellular and molecular processes of tolerance, dependence and withdrawal, but we still have little knowledge of the compulsive drug use neural substrates and their extraordinary persistence. Here we evaluate the evidence for the probability that temptation and its persistence are centered on a pathological usurping of molecular mechanisms normally involved in memory. Many abused drugs produce tolerance, sensitization, reliance and addiction. Of those consequences, addiction (in spite of adverse consequences, compulsive substance use) was the most difficult to study. It is proposed that addiction and its persistence derive from a pathological abrogation of the molecular mechanisms typically involved in memory. Tolerance, sensitization and dependence (which contribute to signs of withdrawal when drug use is stopped) alone do not describe drug addiction or late repetitions long after dropouts are terminated. Relapses can be caused by signals previously linked to drug use.

Drug addiction and brain

Drug addiction is a persistent brain disorder, and it can cause you to search for drugs compulsively even if you are aware of the adverse effects that can induce them. The decision to take drugs is initially voluntary. So, when someone offers you drugs, you can easily say that you'd like to try them, or you might refuse, and that's not going to have any ill effect. When taking drugs for a prolonged period, the addiction sets in and without signs of withdrawal, you can no longer resist the drugs. What tends to cause these symptoms, and why is it so difficult to quit drug use? When you are taking drugs, the way, your brain works changes. It will change to make you unable to withstand the impulse to take drugs; you might feel you need them. Because of this, many people seeking medical help have a difficult time leaving drugs. There's much more to story behind what's happening to the brain, and you should be aware of a lot of improvements.

When you are taking drugs, the chemicals in the drugs enter the brain and continue their journey to change the chemical makeup of your brain. Such chemicals disturb the communication cycle, ensuring that your nerve cells will not receive information, process information or send information the way they should be. Drugs cause that to occur in two ways. First, a drug can mimic the brain's natural chemicals, which will deceive the body into reacting differently. For example, if the drug emulates serotonin, the body may react with euphoria. Additionally, drugs can over-stimulate the part of the brain that thinks it has been rewarded; that means you'll feel good about it when you're taking the drug. If you're always good at taking it, then you're more likely to want to do it again.

Different drugs have different ways of working. For example, marijuana imitates the neurotransmitters and lets the brain send the rest of the body an abnormal message. Such messages usually make the drug user feel happy or other good feelings. Cocaine releases and prevents reabsorption of large volumes of certain neurotransmitters in the nerve cells. If it is a chemical like dopamine or serotonin, when that happens, you will feel very happy and relaxed. If it is a chemical such as adrenaline that is activated, during the time the medication is working, you are likely to be nervous and anxious. The problem with such drugs is that they don't always evoke the same response. The brain is intelligent; it also begins to want most of them to get the same feeling when it knows it will receive large quantities of feel-good chemicals. This is usually referred to as tolerance and the risks and consequences of drug abuse contributing to hospitalization and death of many abusers. After the first time you take a drug, you will build a tolerance which means you will need to raise your dose constantly in order for you to experience the same.

During the drug abuse, the brain endures long-term changes. You will have diminished cognitive function if the brain has to continue to compensate for the loss or modification of glutamate, a chemical that lets you focus. Ultimately, you will have a hard time thinking and knowing the circumstances you 're in. You may be responding more slowly than average or delaying the reflexes. Drugs change brain areas which control important things such as judgment. It will all be influenced by decision making, behavior control, and things like memory or learning skills. When all of these aspects are changed, even though it is harmful, a drug user may be compelled to consume more and more of the drug.

Many people might not be as easily addicted as others, and many factors are responsible for that. It is necessary to realize, though, that taking drugs while a teenager can have more severe consequences. This is because puberty is a period of development where the brain is evolving and developing; at that level, changes made to drugs could be irreversible.

3.3 Addictions and behavioral perspectives

While most people are acquainted with substance addiction, studies show that a person can also develop a behavioral addiction. A behavioral addiction–or process addiction, as is sometimes referred to –is identical to a substance dependence because the individual becomes ultimately dependent upon the pleasant feelings (e.g. gambling) bring about and begins to behave compulsively to reach this level over and over again. A person may be diagnosed with behavioral addiction if they show a lack of self-control over behavior, including reversal of behavior despite negative work or social relationship consequences. Researchers have identified certain common behaviors which could lead to addiction.

- Social media and cell phone.
- Exercise
- Eating and Food.
- Gambling.
- Internet
- Love and relations.
- Masturbation and Pornography.
- Sex.
- Shopping.
- Video games

Effects of addiction on human behavior and personality

Drugs and alcohol influence the behavior of an individual is nothing new. Addiction not only alters personality but also influences the personal and professional relations of the individual and other important life facets. Once caught up in addiction, whether it is linked to drugs or alcohol, victims often show a completely different personality; nothing like what they used to be until the addiction took over. There are many obvious signs of drug addiction one can see in a struggling person. It is not unusual to see those struggling from drug and alcohol addiction become angry over small issues, behaving over seemingly minor things, becoming hostile overall, or even acting differently altogether. Drugs and alcohol have been found to intensify a person's behavior. Individuals who already have violent tendencies may become incredibly violent when under the influence of drugs or alcohol, yet it is common for the person struggling to find nothing wrong with their behavior, and instead fall into the perception that they act or perform better when under the influence.

Upon consuming alcohol, introverts may become more social and friendlier, as they may find that alcohol helps them to ignore their problems and complexes. While the addict or their friends may see this as a positive sign, the fact is that in the long run, the increased dependency on alcohol harms the individual The explanation for this is that when a person uses addictive substances, these substances cause a feeling of elation or euphoria, and the' high,' after drugs or alcohol, is hidden from all feelings of pain and anxiety. But when the alcohol or drug effect is gone, the person finds himself craving the same feeling of pleasure and euphoria once again, and this is when addiction becomes a serious problem.

Most Visible Addictive Personality Traits and Behaviors

Lying: This is the most common trait of personality shown by people who are fighting with addictions. It is not easy to lose faith in them when you've trusted someone for years–and people with problems with alcohol and drug abuse will easily get away with their lies. They bother lying, as they must now cover their actual surroundings when asked' where have you been for so long?'. Those struggling with addiction often spend huge sums of money managing their addiction, which is something they may want to keep from their loved ones. Unfortunately, lying increases with greater addiction.

Manipulative: Since the person struggling is taking part in something that society, their family or their friends may not accept, they may tend to be manipulative. Once they're found abusing drugs or alcohol, they immediately kick in the art of manipulation An individual struggling with addiction can come up with a variety of excuses and convincing lies, insisting that they no longer see their drug dealers, that they have already begun rehabilitation therapy, and it was just a one-off with the friends and not a common occurrence, or that their drug of choice enables them to perform better in their profession. The individual will often be able to manipulate them easily since their dear ones trust them.

Abusive: When addiction is not managed at some point in time, then the person struggling may begin to become violent and abusive with the loved ones. The other half is generally made to bear the brunt of their partner's addiction, whether married or in a relationship. Since someone who is constantly struggling with addiction is being asked to change their ways, they continue to interpret the people around them as harmful or spiteful.

Violent: It's not unusual for those who struggle with addiction to become angry when they feel annoyed about avoiding their substance abuse or seeking professional care because of the constant guidance of loved ones. They become so concerned with their addiction or persecute the feeling of pleasure that they can harm the people around them physically or emotionally. If people who are struggling with addiction see those around them as trying to get around them and their addiction, they could also be seriously endangered by the victims of addiction.

Forgetful: Drug and alcohol abuse directly affects a person's brain; therefore, it's very common for them to be distracted, to the point where they can't remember what they've done–particularly when they're under control. In some cases, a person's memory may be so compromised by drug or alcohol addiction that they may not even remember the conversation you had with them earlier in the day. They will deny anything instantly and depict you as a liar and a stupid.

Secretive: Since they are well informed that their substance abuse will be hated upon in their friends and family circle, individuals that try to hide and become discreet when it comes to their newly discovered habit, which inevitably becomes an addiction with time. Furthermore, addiction victims may not necessarily tell you where they're going, the people they're spending their time with and their day plans. They may fear that if their family and friends come to know about their addiction, they can either disown them or push them to seek medical help to overcome their issues with substance abuse. All the above behavioral changes in the personality of a person may be destructive to the individual's overall health and well-being, including mental health, physical health, and social health. If we mention social well-being, this has to do with the individual's personal status within their community, which can affect their relationship with the people around them. People do not usually like associations with violence issues, and their relatives can avoid any contact with them.

Personal health taking a worse turn: There is a close relationship between addiction and individual health. Addiction, whether it is drug addiction or alcoholism does no harm to those who are addicted or affected When comparison to a personality disorder, the addiction gradually often begins to take effect on a person's physical well-being. The addict is mentally and physically imbalanced owing to excessive use of toxic and dangerous drugs. However, when an addict is ignored or poorly treated by his family and society because of the addiction, it tends to affect them, which in effect leads to problems with emotional health, and then also physical problems. Those who have to deal with drugs and euphoria are so obsessed that the priority they have to find more drugs in their lives to help them achieve the high dream. They lose focus which prevents them from performing even the most basic tasks, such as daily eating or sleeping. It adds the pressures of the already weakened immune system and the overall physical health of such person is broken down.

Loss of personal reputation: Culture has been looking at substance abuse over the years. Many struggling with addiction suffer as a result of their dishonesty, cheating, forgetful, deceptive, threatening, and clandestine actions from loss of reputation. People tend not to like them and view them in a disrespectful way.

Worsening School / University Performance: Some of the most visible changes in someone who suffers from addiction are lack of concentration and loss of interest, especially in individuals of school age. The decline in schooling and eventually, the withdrawal from school or college is a problem among drug and alcohol abuse students. When going through such a groundbreaking period, the person struggling does not learn how to deal with addiction.

Negative Impacts on Professional Life: Someone who suffers also goes through a decline in performance in their workplace This can adversely affect the life of a person and in some situations also affects the lives of those people who rely on them, such as dependent members of the family. People tend to look at and mistreat those who suffer against abuse Addiction is not only restricted to personal harm, but it also affects the view of the individual by society and what other people think about the addict. Generally, people who work with drug abusers constantly complain about the interruptions they endure or the potential hazards arising from the addiction of their co-workers.

Weakened relationships with family and friends: One of the most vulnerable areas is the weakening of relationships with family and friends. Whether it's with family or friends, the addiction of a person leads to fragile and broken bonds. Someone who often, and sometimes very clearly, struggles with addictions hides their weaknesses and becomes very courageous about their drug or alcohol addiction. They even sometimes separate themselves from their families or from the society in which they live just to escape the questions Lies become the simplest way to hide bad habits from one another. Forgetfulness, deception, deceit, abusiveness, minimal-stress tolerance, hypocrisy, and selfishness build a multitude of home issues, contributing to partnership deterioration.

Involvement in criminal and anti-social acts: "Alcohol is a factor in today's 40% of all violent crimes and is linked to drugs and crime" says National Council on Alcohol and Drug Dependence. It is found that both drug addiction and alcoholism lead to irresponsible behavior on the part of a person and their increased tendency to take unnecessary risks. Similarly, while people may fall into criminal traps under the influence of drugs and alcohol, they often engage in acts that are socially or ethically unacceptable. We continue to be seen as a social outcast, often rack up criminal charges daily.

Human behavior, health and Addiction: Addiction, human behavior, and health They have heard and acknowledged from the above debate that drugs and alcohol can have significant, harmful effects on people. But how often did we try to figure out the reason for a person's addiction?

How addiction impacts the mental effects of the brain: Addiction leads someone to act unpredictably. The starkest reason is that drugs and alcohol are destructive of the brain when a person's brain under the influence is filled by dopamine, a neurotransmitter that resides in the parts of the brain that regulates activity, inspiration, human emotion, and enjoyment feelings. A person experiences periods of intense pleasure and happiness when taking drugs or alcohol, but when the same euphoria feelings face-off, the person is forced to seek more drugs and alcohol to recreate that same moment of joy. As the need to be in a condition of euphoria becomes greater, the patient becomes more and more addicted. Unfortunately, a person who has pursued the initial height has grown into a vicious cycle of drug abuse slowly but surely. Constant abuse changes essential brain activity over time and causes the brain to prefer addiction over other primary tasks Because the brain is concerned with drugs or alcohol, someone who is struggling with addiction is going through dramatic psychological and behavioral changes. People who suffer from addiction sometimes transform into a whole different person.

Corrective measures: The first step towards a safer life is to recognize that you are consuming and addict to drugs or alcohol. It's not easy to overcome addiction, but it's not difficult either. One thing you should do is to speak with friends and family who matter for you and support you. Be truthful about your abuse and addiction with them and ask them how they can help you in your life throughout this difficult time. It's the option whether to receive professional medical help or undertake self-treatment. Over practice, you'll be able to know what's best for you. Ask people, research your paths to free yourself from the vicious cycle. Above all: don't give up. You will survive with enough tenacity and determination and continue to live a fulfilled life. Likewise, anytime you find out a loved one is dealing with a struggle with drug or alcohol abuse, it's a scary feeling. In these crisis situations, leaning on the people nearest to you is crucial. Do your homework and get recovery education to help you throughout the cycle. It's also important to understand how a family can respond with addictions. Understanding what care to go for in the recovery centers is important for you. It is not easy to talk to the one who is hurting, but then again, something as basic as communicating can save their lives. Don't give up, and you are going to make it through. Note, it is likely that someone who suffers from addiction will fully recover and go on living perfect, natural lives.

3.4 How we can treat the addictions? / Treatments

Addictive disorders are a series of physical and psychological damage disorders. To break the cycle of addiction, treatment is necessary. Moreover, addiction is difficult to treat as a chronic disease, which needs ongoing care. When addicted, an abnormal desire for alcohol and drugs develops in your body. Going without outcomes in dreadful signs of withdrawal such as anxiety trembling, sweating, nausea and depression. There is no solution for addiction, and it doesn't work just by telling a person to quit. Yet fortunately, there are successful ways to treat addiction. Which treatment is effective depends on different factors and conditions, such as addiction severity and whether mental disorders (such as anxiety or depression) are associated with it? Here's a brief look at how to treat addiction:

First step

The first step in rehabilitation is to understand that the use of drugs has become a problem in life that disrupts the quality of life of individuals. This can be due to impairment in schooling, work, social, recreational or other essential functional fields. Once a person understands a substance's negative impact on their life, a diverse range of treatments is available. A person suffering from an addictive disorder needs access to treatment. The treatment can last for most people for the rest of their lives. They will have to refrain on a lifetime basis from the substance, which can be challenging. Treatment strategies for addictive disorders often satisfy the patient's needs. Addiction treatment options depend on a number of factors including the type of addiction disorder the duration and intensity of use and its impact on the person. Any health complications that have occurred such as liver disease in an individual with a condition with alcohol or respiratory problems in people with a substance addiction that has been smoked will also be treated or recommended for treatment. There are many treatment options available, and a variety of solutions will be offered to most people suffering from addiction. None of the addictive disorder therapies works for every patient. Common operations may include a combination of inpatient and outpatient programmers, psychological counselling, self-help groups and medication.

Detoxification

Normally detoxification is the first step in the treatment. It means removing a substance from the body and restricting responses to withdrawal. 80% of patients in the treatment centers use drugs to minimize withdrawal symptoms. If an individual is addicted to more than one drug, they may sometimes need medications for each to reduce the symptoms of withdrawal. The NSS-2 Bridge electronic device was made available in 2017 to reduce the removal of opiates. The device sits behind the ear and releases electric pulses which can trigger some nerves to relieve withdrawal symptoms.

Behavioral therapies and counselling

It is the most common method of treatment after detoxification. Depending on the individual's needs, therapy may occur on a one-to-one, group or family basis. The frequency of sessions typically reduces gradually over time when the symptoms are better at the start of treatment. Specific treatment types include cognitive-behavioral therapy, which allows people to recognize and modify ways of thinking associated with the use of drugs. Multi-dimensional family counselling, aimed at improving the role of the family around a teenager with a substance-related illness motivational interview, maximizing the willingness of people to make changes and modifications to perform motivational opportunities for abstention via constructive enhancements. The first-ever smartphone application, reSET ®, was approved by the United States Food and Drug Administration (FDA) in 2017 as safe for use alongside outpatient monitoring of marijuana, cocaine, alcohol and stimulant use disorders. In contrast to the behavior's characteristic of addiction, certain types of treatment for addictive disorders concentrate on the underlying reason for the addictive condition.

Rehabilitation programmers

Long-term treatment programs can be highly effective for substance-related and addictive disorders and generally concentrate on staying drug-free and resuming activity within social, professional and family responsibilities. Fully certified residential facilities are present to administer a 24-hour care program, provide a secure housing environment and provide any medical treatments or assistance that may be necessary. A few types of facilities can provide a supportive atmosphere, including:

Short-term residential treatment: It focuses on detoxification and educating a patient in a therapeutic group through intense therapy for a longer period of time.

Therapeutic communities: A person seeking long-term care for severe forms of addiction disorder would stay in residence with on-site workers and others in rehabilitation for between 6 and 12 months. The community and staff play an important role in the healing and improvements in attitudes and behaviors.

Recovery housing: This provides a monitored, short-term stay in housing to help people take on commitments and adapt to a different, independent life without continued use of substances. Recovery housing comprises advice on how to handle finances and find work, as well as providing a person's connection during the final phases of recovery and community support.

Self-help groups: These can help the recovering person meet those with the same addictive disorder that often boosts motivation and diminishes isolation feelings. They can also provide useful information, of education and community. Examples include Anonymous Alcoholics (AA), and Anonymous Narcotics (NA). People struggling against other addictions may find out about self-help groups in their neighborhoods either by finding on the internet or by requesting information from a doctor or nurse.

Medications

If a person recovers from a drug-related disorder and its complications, he or she could take medicine continuously. However, people more often use drugs to treat withdrawal symptoms during detoxification. The prescription varies according to the drug to which the person is addicted. The longer-term use of medications helps to reduce hunger and avoid fatigue or a return to addiction after treatment. Medication is not a stand-alone drug treatment and should be followed by other forms of treatment such as psychotherapy. Special treatment is required for addiction to the following substances.

Alcohol: The following medications may be used by people with alcohol use disorder to minimize cravings and withdrawal symptoms, including naltrexone: this prevents the action of drug receptors in the brain that generate rewarding and euphoric impacts when a person consumes alcohol and lowers the risk of relapsing. Although not effective in treatment for all people, in some cases, it has a tremendous impact on prohibition.

Acamprosate, or Campral: This may reduce symptoms of long-term withdrawal, including insomnia, anxiety and a general sense of dissatisfaction known as dysphoria. This has a more positive effect on individuals suffering from severe alcohol and addiction disorders.

Disulfiram, or Antabuse: This is a medication that interferes with alcohol breakdown, leading to harmful effects such as facial redness, feeling tired, and an irregular heartbeat should the person attempt to consume alcohol in recovery. This serves as a dissuasive to people with high levels of encouragement for rehabilitation.

Other medications may be prescribed by doctors and recovery practitioners to treat other potential mental disorders, including depression and anxiety, which may be a cause or effect of drug-related disorders. Participants in treatment programs should also undergo infectious disease tests that could have arisen from certain high-risk conditions associated with their addictive disorders such as Aids, hepatitis and tuberculosis.

Twelve-step programs: In addition to (or after) professional treatment, 12-step programs can assist addicted individuals. These include Anonymous Alcoholics, Narcotics Anonymous and Anonymous Cocaine. The goal is to attain prohibition for people. People accept having a disease commit it to greater power and participate actively in all 12 steps.

Exercising: Evidence has shown that exercise helps with smoking cessation, in addition to traditional therapy, because it improves mood and reduces stress. Experts think that it can also assist with other addictions.

Therapies

CBT- Cognitive behavioral therapy:

Cognitive-behavioral therapy, or CBT, tells you how to interpret moods, emotions and circumstances in which drug cravings are fired up. A therapist may teach you how to stop such triggers. You must begin to substitute harmful feelings and thoughts with healthier ones which will help you stay safe. The techniques you will be acquiring can last a lifetime, so this is a valuable method of treatment. But not all the therapists are trained in techniques for cognitive behavioral therapy.

DBT – Dialectical Behavioral Treatment: Dialectical behavioral treatment is successful in people struggling to control feelings and having self-harm or suicidal thoughts. The therapy emphasizes that unpleasant thoughts, feelings or behaviors are accepted to allow individuals to overcome them. DBT includes relaxation exercises, such as yoga, which help patients become more aware of their thoughts and feelings. To condone self-destructive thoughts or urges, they develop skills such as controlled breathing and muscle relaxation. The aim is to reduce the severity and frequency of self-harming actions and to promote healthy change.

The Matrix model: The Matrix model gives a structure for maintaining abstinence among people suffering from stimulant abuse. It is used mainly in people suffering from heroin or cocaine abuse. Matrix-based treatment includes a range of evidence-based treatments that encourage the reduction of relapse and facilitate involvement in family therapy, schooling, and support groups. The therapy sessions usually provide comprehensive worksheets or reference notes for the participant. The therapist is a counsellor and mentor who maintains a supportive therapeutic relationship and encourages behavioral change. In the individual, the therapist encourages confidence and self-worth and prevents antagonistic contact. The Matrix model, however, does include drug testing.

Contingency management therapy: This technique provides you with constructive opportunities to stay clean. Services and goods vouchers or benefits are popular in a more restrictive care environment.

Motivational interviewing: Therapists aim to empower you in this process to encourage you to sustain your prohibition from drugs or alcohol. If you are prompted by family love or return to work, these problems may become the subject of your treatment.

Couples and family therapy: An addiction not only affects your life; it is transforming your whole family. Successful treatment needs strong familial and friendly relationships. Diverse therapy approaches include your mother and other members of your family.

Why try therapy for families or couples?

- Family members can be a strong driving force for change.

- Including these can increase your chances of staying in therapy.

- They will continue repairing the harm the relapse has created in their lives.

Studies show that family therapy leads to lower recessions, greater family satisfaction, and helps children with addicted parents to manage.

Yoga, meditation and mindfulness: Yoga is an exercise in which synchronized breathing, and body postures are stressed to encourage physical strength, relaxation and serenity. Clinical trials concerning yoga and mindfulness found the therapies to be effective complements for the prevention and treatment of addiction.

A meta-analysis of mediation studies published in the quarterly Alcoholism Therapy showed that the method could reduce stress, distress, tobacco smoking, and alcohol and drug abuse. Furthermore, a clinical trial published in the Journal of Professional and Clinical Psychology on relaxation meditation found yoga was a practical and effective therapy for drug abuse and chronic pain.

Animal Therapy: Animals are involved in various therapies for addiction. Patients come into contact with horses during equine therapy which is one of the most famous animal-assisted therapies. The horses provide feedback via nonverbal signals. Patients try to understand their own feelings and surmount negative emotions, including frustration and anxiety. Other therapies constitute people who voluntarily support animals during traditional treatment sessions in shelters or with animals in recovery. Research indicates that animal or pet-assisted rehabilitation will increase a patient's participation in recovery and willingness to discuss some history of trauma or misuse of drugs. Animal-assisted treatment also can reduce stress, anxiety and fear.

Acupuncture therapy: In order to stimulate healing, acupuncture professionals insert fine needles into the body. Acupuncture is a unique treatment option at multiple rehabilitation facilities, and people follow up benefits from acupuncture in self-help programs too. A report issued in the Archives of Internal Medicine of patients recovering from cocaine addiction found patients allocated to acupuncture therapy were more likely to refrain from cocaine use. Another report issued in the American Journal of Public Health found that acupuncture considerably improved cessation rates for tobacco smoking.

Music therapy: Music therapy strategies include emotionally based lyrical interpretation, songwriting, art playing, and ad-libbing music. Patients indulge emotions, intentions and barriers through lyrics and melody during music therapy. Music therapy research has found songwriting can encourage healthy change, drumming can facilitate healing, and dancing can reduce stress, anxiety, and depression symptoms. A report issued in the Drug & Alcohol Review found that a patient's willingness for treatment was positively related to musical therapy.

Art therapy: Art therapy Patients portray themselves through art therapy by designing, painting, sculpting, or creating art books. Art therapy methods also include anxiety painting, in which people paint through periods of high distress, and making sketches of incidents: depictions of events that occurred during drug abuse. In art therapy, some therapists emphasize extrapolation and deliberation as therapeutic techniques. Art therapy studies indicate it can reduce denial, avoidance of treatment, and shame. It can also be used to make group discussions easier and to motivate change.

Takeaway

Substance-related disorders are serious, complex diseases which require intensive, prolonged treatment. The type of drug involved, and the extent of the addiction will determine the treatment plan. Treatment also begins with detoxification, using medications to alleviate symptoms of withdrawal while a substance exits the system. Various types of behavioral counselling and therapy may also support treatment, thereby helping to deprogram certain behaviors and drug-related circumstances. Occasionally, a person begins a rehabilitation program for 6 to 12 months in a different facility. They may then stay in monitored housing while they are readjusting to handle the finances and find jobs. Some medications may also serve to manage symptoms of prolonged withdrawal and support mental stability in some individuals.

Chapter 4: How to conquer panic, fear and anxiety

Fear plays a major role in our life but in a negative way. One who can stop all his/her fears can easily achieve his/her life goals. Many individuals feel frustrated with anxiety and want to avoid situations that could intimidate or disturb them. This chain can be hard to break, but it can come in many forms. You will continue to feel less afraid and scared, so you don't stop living. We can't ignore any source of stress or remove it in our lives. However, we should learn safer ways to respond to them. Another method is to use a strategy first introduced by cardiologist Dr Herbert Benson, author of the Harvard Medical School Special Health in the 1970s, to use the' relaxation response.' The response to relaxation is the opposite of stress. It is a condition of deep rest which can, in several cases, be activated. You create a calm well as required with regular workouts. If you live at high-stress levels, you place your whole well-being at risk. Stress influences your mental well-being and physical wellbeing. Proper stress management allows you to break the stress of your life, to make you feel happier, healthier and more productive. People with a good mind lead a healthier, happier life.

4.1 Mind relaxing techniques to conquer fear, panic worry

One of the strongest feelings is fear. This affects your mind and body very strongly. For example, if we're in a fire or are being assaulted, fear will create strong signals of reaction. It can also take effect in the event of non-hazardous activities such as tests, public speech, a job, date, or even a group. It is a normal reaction to a danger that is perceivable or actual. Anxiety is a term for certain kinds of worries, which typically have to do with thinking of a future threat or something wrong, instead of right now. Anxiety and fear can last for a while and then pass, but it can also last for a lot longer. In some situations, they can take over your life and influence you're eating, sleeping, thinking, driving, having a great time or even going to work or school. You can stop doing things you need or want to do, and that affects your health as well.

Some people are overwhelmed with fear and want to prevent situations that could make them afraid or distressed. This loop can be difficult to break, but many forms are possible. You should learn to feel less scared and be afraid so that you don't stop living.

Relaxation techniques seem to be strategies for stress and anxiety reduction. Such strategies can also help manage panic disorder symptoms and help a person to panic. Relaxation strategies are used to control combat-or-flight reaction, which is often caused by anxiety disturbances in individuals. The fight-or-flight reflex causes extreme reactions that normally ignore some specific threat to the environment. Of starters, people with agoraphobia often fear that they will flee in a panic attack from crowded spaces or open spaces. The reaction to battle or flight also triggers annoyance signs, such as elevated heart tempo, rapid breathing and excessive sweating. Calming strategies have been shown to have a reverse impact on the body by enhancing calming responses, decreasing heart pressures, dropping negative thoughts and growing self-esteem and solving skills.

Some best relief strategies for anxiety are listed here. It is crucial that you exercise them often and at moments when you don't seem too interested and make the most of those relaxation techniques. Choose a technique that fits your lifestyle and appeals to you. Take approximately 5-10 minutes a day to do it. You are trained to use the strategies whenever there are fear and distress by regular practice.

Exercises of Deep Breathing. Breathing exercises underlie many other methods of calming and are easy to learn. Such exercises help you to respire slowly and deeply, so you can feel relaxed. Air treatments have been known to purify you so that you remain invigorated and renewed. Deep respiration often emphasizes on the respiration cycle, thereby calming your mind and allowing you to control the pace of your breath. These exercises can help to minimize muscle tension and improve other common panic symptoms, such as a decrease in quick cardiac rates and shortness of breath.

Visualization. Visualizing is an effective way of relieving stress and worry. You use your imagination through visualization to imagine yourself in a peaceful and relaxed environment, like on a seaside or in a flower-covered wilderness. Visualization serves to soothe both body and mind. You will eventually allow your body and mind to feel like you're there by just gazing at yourself in a rejuvenating environment. PMR is an efficient anxiety management strategy, which decreases discomfort in the entire body, thereby relaxing any troubling feelings. PMR means that different muscle types are stretched and activated to reduce bodily pressure. You can also relax and ease the mind by focusing your attention on making the pain flow throughout the body. PRM may help you realize if your muscles are constrained and physical discomfort, which contributes to your anxiety can be more easily released.

Meditation and Yoga. Some consider meditation and yoga effective for decreasing anxiety and stress. Yoga will help you alleviate anxiety, enhance focus and relax in the entire body. Meditation can also be used alone or in yoga and is also an effective way to make you feel more relaxed, calmer and concentrated.

These relaxing methods can be used to alleviate and reduce anxiety in the morning and to start feeling refreshed during the day. At the end of the day, they can also be used to alleviate some stress and tension.

Relaxation techniques & self-care methods. When incorporated into your relative wellness as well as self-care practices, relaxation techniques maybe even more effective. Self-care approaches consist of behaviors that improve your health, including your personal wellbeing' mental, physical, spiritual or regulatory elements. It can be effective to look at the general self-care habits if you are dealing with panic disorder. Such methods include the application of your relaxation techniques, social support, recovery and physical fitness criteria.

Some other strategies to conquer fear and anxiety are:

Discourage avoidance. Face it, is the only way to confront terror. This stops us from progressing — this leads us to panic. Therapists can be helpful and help us build our approaches to eliminate them. When you encounter loss, engaging with a therapist is especially important to create a safe space to confront your anxiety and to build up your memories. One approach in milder cases is to use methods like awareness therapy and cope with the emerging. You just have to sit silently and enjoy the moment. Recognize it if fear and anxiety occur. See it rising. Find out how the body feels. Look at it as it is; do not seek to alter it.

Encourage positivity. Fear helps us to note and recall negative events that reinforce our perception of the environment as a frightening place. We will work to change this by knowing consciously what is nice — the joy that we get when we see someone we value, the enjoyment of a beautiful day, nature's beauty, the fun of a journey, laughter in a circumstance. Positivity extends our viewpoints, according to studies by Barbara Fredrickson, and we actually have a broader view that presents us with more opportunities. And the more constructive we become, the more endurance it generates, which helps us to work even in difficult times.

Seek meaning. Because we realize it, anxiety will disrupt our sense of the world. Those with injuries may also have real losses, causing them to doubt the value of their lives. Trauma survivors often feel guilty of what occurred, thinking, illogically, that they might have avoided it, and this embarrassment can also contribute to questions of their importance. Nonetheless, it is necessary to rediscover a sense of meaning, irrespective of distress or trauma. An 80-year analysis of longevity-enhanced variables showed that those who adjust to healthy habits after abuse find meaning and maintaining a sense of global security in the traumatic experience.

Get help. Fear may also lead us to feel irrelevant. The initiative for longevity has shown that the quality of their social interactions is one of the primary predictors in the survival of individuals with abuse in their lives. This is for numerous reasons. Family and friends will allow us to evaluate the danger objectively. They are more assured that we can solve problems with the help of others. So emotionally, getting next to a loved one calms us and eliminates fighting or the flight reaction.

Go to nature for a walk. In nature, it reduces fear and fear, increasing pleasant feelings as the new area of naturally based therapies shows. Look at the beauty of nature, with terms like peace, grace, joy, optimism, and liveliness you explain your emotions. Being related to nature not only increases people's emotional sensation; it also reduces blood pressure, heart rhythm, cortisol, and stress hormone production— all signs of stress and fear. To locate a Park or a Greenspace and go on a hike or a trip whether you battle worries or anxiousness. The physical activity will also improve the mindset, along with the restorative benefits of nature.

4.2 Stress management

You put your whole wellbeing at risk if you live with high-stress levels. Your mental wellbeing and physical health are influenced by tension. This reduces the ability for learning, functioning and enjoying life simply. It may seem that you can't do anything about stress. There are no more hours a day and the work and family obligations will always be overwhelming. The expenses do not stop coming. But you control it a lot more than you could think. Appropriate stress management enables you to break your life's stress so that you can be more happy, healthy and productive. The ultimate aim is to exist in harmony, with time for work, friends, recreation and leisure— the ability to hold on and face challenges. Nonetheless, stress management is not all-in-one. That's why experimenting and finding out which works best for you is important. You can do that with the following hints on stress management.

Tip 1: Identify your life's causes of stress

Stress management begins with the identification of stress sources in your life. It's not as simple as it sounds. Although it is easy to recognize major stress factors such as changes in employment, movement or divorce, it may be more difficult to identify the sources of chronic stress. It is all too easy to ignore the contribution made by your own ideas, feelings and behavior to daily stress levels. Yes, you might be conscious that you are constantly concerned about working time constraints, but perhaps it's the frustration and not the actual demands for work, which cause stress.

Looking closely at your behavior, your mentality and your reasons to define the real causes of tension:

- you claim stress to be situational ("I have just a million-stuff going right now").
- Would you describe stress as an essential component of your job or home life ("Things are always insane here," "I have such a lot of nervous energy, this is all")?
- Do you blame or consider your stress to be totally normal and unusual?

You cannot control your stress level unless you take responsibility for the part that you perform in generating or sustaining it.

Tip 2: 4 A's of stress management practice

Stress is an automated reaction of your nervous system, but some stressors occur at routine times: for instance, your work commute, your managers' meeting or family reunions. You could either make the situation better or adjust the response while managing such repetitive stressors. It is helpful to consider four A's when determining which option; you can choose for a given scenario: avoid, alter, adapt or accept them.

Avoid stress that is unnecessary

It is not good for health to avoid a stressful situation that wants to be addressed, but you might be surprised by the amount of stressors that can be eliminated in your life. Understand and stick to your limits. Learn how to say "no." If you take in more than you can manage in your professional or personal life, it is a healthy prescription for stress. Differ from the' may' and' musts' and tell' no' or take on too many, if necessary. Ignore people who are stressing you. If anyone creates stress in your life, restrict your contact with that person or end your partnership. Control away from the surroundings. If you're concerned about the night television, turn the TV off. Choose a longer however less-travelled path if you are stressed. You can go shopping online if it's an unpleasant task for the market. Pare the set of to-dos. Analyze your calendar, responsibilities and daily activities. If you have too much on the board, reduce or delete things that are not really important at the bottom of the list.

Alter the situation.

If a stressful scenario can't be avoided, try to change it. This often involves changing your way of communication and working in your everyday life. Rather than bottling them, share your thoughts. If you are bothered by someone or something, feel more confident and express your thoughts freely and politely. When you have an interview and your friend comes home, inform him front that you have only five mins to talk. Unless you express your thoughts, resentment is created, and stress is enhanced. You are ready to compromise. You'll be able to do the same if you expect somebody to alter their behavior. You will have a reasonable opportunity to find a perfect middle ground if you're at least willing to bend slightly. Build a realistic strategy. Each work and thus, no play are a burnout recipe. Attempt to find a balance between work & family life, social and solitary habits, everyday tasks and downtimes.

Adaptability for the stressor.

Alter yourself if you can't change the source of stress. Through changing your beliefs and mindset, you will adjust to stressful conditions and recover your sense of control. Problems are reframing. Try to look more favorably at stressful situations. Look at this as an opportunity to stop and group yourself, pay attention to your favorite radio station or spend some time alone instead of smoking about a traffic jam! Take the unpleasant situation into account. Consider how relevant it's going to be in the long term. In a month, will that matter? Two years? A year? Is that really worth getting angry? Spend time and energy elsewhere if the response is no. Set the standards. Raise the values. The main source of preventable stress is perfectionism. Stop to set up by claiming excellence for disappointment. Give yourself and others reasonable standards and strive to be all right with "nice enough." Take a moment to reflect on everything that you love into your life, including your own good things and talents, while tension is coming down. You will keep it in perspective with this simple strategy.

Accept things that you can't change.

There are certain causes of stress. Stressors such as a friend's death, a serious disease or a global crisis cannot be avoided or modified. In these situations, acknowledging things as they are is the best way to deal with pain. Acceptance is challenging because, in the long term, it's better than raging, you can't change against a case. Don't try to keep uncontrollable under control. Many things in life, especially the conduct of others, is beyond our control. Instead of stressing them, focus on things, like how you respond to challenges, that you can manage. Look upwards. Try to view them as tools for personal development when dealing with major challenges. Reflect onto them and learn from your mistakes if your own poor decisions have led to a stressful situation. Learn to forget; try to forgive. Understand that we live and make errors in an imperfect world. Let go of the fury and resentment. Release yourself by loving and moving on from negative energies. Share your opinion. It can be very cathartic to share what you are doing, particularly if nothing can be done to change the serious situation. Speak to a trustworthy partner or schedule a therapy date.

Tip 3: Keep going.

The last thing you likely have to do when you're stressed is get up and practice. Yet physical exercise is an incredible stress relief, and you need not be an athlete or live in a fitness room for hours. Exercise launches endorphins which make you feel comfortable and can help to distract you from your everyday concerns.

Although the regular exercise takes you the most, it's all right to increase your level of fitness gradually. In the course of a day, even very little activities could add up. The first stage is to push and get up. Take a walk or ride to the food store. Use the steps at home or at work rather than a lift. Park your car at the end of your lot and stroll on the rest of the way Partner with a fitness buddy to support one another as you work out Play Table or an active Table. There are a few easy ways to add activity into your daily schedule:

While almost every form of physical exercise can help reduce tension and stress, rhythmic exercises are especially effective. The calming power of mindful movement. Walking, biking, surfing, juggling, spinning, tai chi and aerobics are all good choices. But make sure it's something you like, whatever you choose, and you will stay with it more likely. During your preparation, make a conscious effort to take care of your body and your physical (and often emotional) emotions while you are running. Focus, for instance, on how to coordinate your respiration with your movements or see how your skin feels air or sunlight. Including this dimension of awareness lets you escape from the loop of negative thoughts, sometimes causing unbearable tension.

Tip 4: Talk with other people.

There is nothing calmer than to spend quality time with someone else who makes you feel comfortable and well understood. The face-to-face interaction, in fact, triggers a flurry of hormones to counter the "fight-or-flight" response of the body. This is the natural stress reliever for nature (as an additional bonus, it also helps to prevent depression and anxiety). Make it a point of communicating with friends and family regularly— and in person. Bear in mind that you don't have to address the depression for people you are talking to. You just have to be good communicators. And don't try to make you think that you look weak or that you are a burden. The confidence should flatter the people who care for you. It just strengthens your bond. In reality, when you're overcome with tension, it's not always a practical mission, but you can strengthen your resilience against life's stressors by creating and retaining a network of friends.

Tip 5: Take your time to fun and relaxation.

You will reduce tension and stress in your life beyond a take-off strategy and a positive attitude by investing "me" time. Don't get so lost in the busy life that you think about your own needs. It's a requirement, not a luxury to nurture yourself. You are in a better place to handle stressful lives if you usually make time to have fun and relaxation.

Set the time to relax aside. Pay attention to relaxation. Do not authorize the interference of other responsibilities. It's time to break free from any duties and recharge your batteries. Create something every day you love. Take the time to go and have fun, whether it's starring, playing the piano, or operating on your motorcycle. Maintain that sense of humor. This requires the ability to laugh. The humor helps your body combat stress in many respects. Take a practice of relaxation. The restlessness of your body, which is opposite of the battle or flight, is intensified by relaxing strategies such as yoga, meditation and hot air. Through practicing and performing these strategies, you can reduce the stress levels and relax and center your minds and bodies.

Tip 6: Better time control.

Bad management of time can cause a great deal of stress. It's difficult to stay calm and focused when you stretch too thin and run behind. Therefore, all the good stuff you should do, including socializing and relaxing, you will be tented to stop or that. The excellent news is that you can do things to achieve a better balance between work and life. Don't give yourself over. Do not plan things for one day or try to fit too much. They forget all too often how long things are going to take. Consider activities a priority. Make a list of activities and address them as seriously as possible. Then do the most important items. If you're particularly uncomfortable or anxious about something, get it through early. This will help the rest of your day more fun. Bridge projects into little steps. Make a step-by-step plan if a major project seems overwhelming. Reflect on one easy step at a time instead of doing it all at once — responsibility for delegates. You do not have to do it yourself, whether at school, at home or at work. Why not let other people carry out the task? Let every small step go of the will to regulate or supervise. In the meantime, you will let go of undue stress.

Tip 7: Keep balance in a healthy lifestyle.

Other healthy life-life choices can increase resistance to stress, in addition to the regular exercise. Stress less women with earbuds in her ears eat healthy food. Well-nurtured people are better able to cope with tension, so be conscious of what you are drinking. Begin the day with breakfast and keep your body and mind focused throughout the day healthy, nutritious meals. Caffeine & sugar should be reduced. Caffeine & sugar transient "gain" is often triggered by a mood and energy drop. You will feel more relaxed and sleeping better by limiting the amount of coffee, soft drinks, chocolate and sugar snacks in your diet.

Avoid drugs, alcohol and cigarettes. Alcohol or medication self-healing may help you escape depression quickly, but the cure is only temporary. Do not prevent or mask the problem; deal with problems with a clear mind, head-on. Have enough food — sufficient sleep power both your mind and your body. Tiredness will raise your stress since it can irrationally end up causing you to think.

Tip 8: Momentarily learning to alleviate stress.

You need to be able to control your stress levels instantly if you are confused from your morning ride, trapped in a tense meeting at work or burned from another conversation with your partner. This is where stress relief falls so easily. It's the deepest breath and use of your sense— what you can see, hear, taste, feel — and a relaxing movement that reduces stress most quickly. You can easily relax and concentrate on a favorite snapshot, scent a particular smell, hear favorite music, taste a piece of gum or embrace a pet, for example. Clearly, not all respond in the same way to each sensual experience. The key to fast stress relief is to test and learn about the distinctive sensory experiences that best work for you.

4.3 Road to a healthy mind

It always is a good time to consider ways of keeping your mind balanced, whether you're 25 or 75. People with a strong mentality lead a happier and healthier existence.

Get a lot of mental workouts.

As a muscle does, the brain may atrophy. Take the tips below to give the mind a daily mental training.

1. You use your brain. There is plenty of expertise up there, so do it. Tasks such as question-solving or the evasion of the mathematical machine are one form of training the mind.

2. Crosswords. Perform the quiz puzzles every day when you have the newspaper. Normally, the week continues on, and the game finishes on Sunday. They become progressively harder. You can find plenty of free crucible puzzles online if you're not getting the newspaper.

3. Scrabble. Play Scrabble professionally or play online with friends. Scrabble is a marvelous way to think about your personality.

4. News. Start with the events of today. Whether you're interested in politics, international affairs, or the own little town gossip, it's holding your mind busy.

5. Read. Read everything, papers, newspapers, cereal box backgrounds. Learning keeps your mind busy, and also you learn new things. However, it is certainly a bonus if you have a depth of your study material.

6. Jigsaws. You need to worry about how the shapes, as well as colors, fit when operating puzzles. Working puzzles' problem-solving skills help keep your mind firm.

7. Films. See a learning movie. Enjoy it. Movies such as the Fountain, Jacob's Ladder, as well as 12 Monkeys, can leave your mind thinking about what you have been watching days later.

8. Word riddles. Solve anagrams, reasoning questions or rebuses, for example. Brainteasers. You will appreciate them with any moment you have a couple of additional minutes.

9. Video games. Who said that video games are time-wasting? Perhaps playing video games may help combat Alzheimer's.

10. Hobbies. Begin a new hobby or get an old, forgotten hobby to flow your creative juices.

Do not forget to work out regularly.

Whether you have a five days fitness training or just a couch potato, regular exercise helps keep your mind and body in place. Exercise enhances blood flow, and the brain oxygenates, so pass.

- Lawn works. Tossing the raspberry, raking leaves or simply collecting the stumps falling into the courtyard all are great ways of exercising.
- Walk your dog. Having dog out to walk will improve your mood and wellbeing–both of which add to a better spirit.
- Swimming. Jump into the lake or go for a great workout at your nearby pool.
- Motorcycle. A relaxed cycling tour via a park or a specific bike route isn't just good for yourself; you will also enjoy the scenery.
- Yoga. Yoga is a great way to make your mind and body move at all times of the day.
- Tai chi. Learn about this ancient movement and extend it to a great beginning every morning.
- Hike. Put a few robust shoes and move. Walking can be as straightforward as walking a public park or visiting the state or national park in a more complicated fashion.
- Dancing. Take lessons in dance. Practice tango or dance on the new line and move your body. So, what you're going to age so sound.
- Tennis. This popular sport will have brain health in its highest form, both mentally and physically.
- Golf. Enjoy a relaxed golf course that helps keep your mind fit for both exercise or social benefits.

Test your brain.

Understanding and trying new things is an excellent way for your brain to stretch. Such concepts will give your mind a true opportunity to practice and bring a whole different dimension to your existence beyond a daily workout.

1. Learn. Be interested in the world around you. When you hear a word that you don't know, see it. You don't know to see a flower? See what it is.

2. Music. Learn how to play music, how to read music, and how to take a class in music theory.

3. Language. Learn the language of another country. Perhaps you can resuscitate this Spanish high school and prepare for a visit to Mexico.

4. Art. Learning a new form of art doesn't require talent, really an interest in learning. Research photographic craft, practice painting or learn how to hop

pottery.

5. Turn sides. Seek to use the less dominant hand for simple activities such as eating and filing. A significant stimulation to the brain is the changing of position.

6. Chess. Choose a chess buddy if you know how to learn to play chess.

7. Career. Is your work fulfilled or detrimental to your health? Think hard when making a switch if it is the latter one.

8. Tour. If you have wanted to explore the now-defunct Road 66 or the remains of Maya, take an excursion. Exploring and changing your norm in different cultures sharpens your mind.

9. Education. Go to school for that degree you want to take. It is a good brain test to study at college.

4.4 People's experiences and proven strategies

Examination, traffic, argument and deadline are all-sufficient to trigger a' fight or escape' response, and to send stress hormones and adrenalin to our bodies. Sometimes a war against the body or a flight can be super-sensitive, and it goes on pressing if there is no real threat. The message comes from the amygdala, part of the brain that has been in charge of battling or escaping for decades. During work, it is great, but it works a little too much occasionally.

The very first thing you should know is to manage anxiety

 If there is no real threat, fight or flight is not appropriate. This ensures that the oxygen & energy supplied to your body are not required. If you can do some type of physical workout to metabolize these chemicals, it will be fantastic–but it won't be possible everywhere. The grow-up of these substances in the body leads to any clinical symptoms of anxiety.

The response to relaxation.

Amygdala has been able to initiate the fighting and the flight response for millions of years more practical than we had to stop, so generally, there is no worry about it that it won't work. We have to persuade the same brain which has heroically acted to protect us in the war or in the ride, to calm their jets because we are all right. The calming approach was specifically designed for this function by its very definition. Harvard cardiologist Dr Herbert Benson has revealed this. The best part of the relaxation response is that it's hardwired in the human brain as well as the fight or the flight response. As hardwired, the relaxing mechanism doesn't have to believe–it works. It is automatic, just like the combat or flight response is automatic, whether or not we need it. When the relaxing mechanism is activated, neurochemicals are immediately sent out, neutralizing the fighting or the flight response. Relief can lower blood pressure, minimize heart rate, decrease pulse rate, decrease blood oxygen and raise brain waves alpha (reliefs).

Monitor your respiration. The clinical signs correlated with short-speed respiration, oxygen over-supply and a faster heart rate reverse while the respiration is regulated. You can do this in a few manners: sit still. Relax, two, three through your nose. Remember until your breathing is in check. Remember to breathe through the nose,' Three, two, three.

- Take your breathing conscious.
- Place your chest with one hand and your stomach with one.
- Respire to fill your stomach.
- Stand momentarily with your heart.
- Slowly breathe out, think about' relaxation,' and feel the belly fall.
- Try to ensure the hand does not travel very much on your stomach.
- Repeat 5 to 10 times, focusing deeply and slowly on breathing.
- Practice regularly–even on the good days–and when you need it, you'll have it.
- Do this by taking a short stop between breathing out and respiring in. Try to slow your breathing down.

1. Workout.

Metabolizing excess hormones but also returning the body to rest will prevent overactivity in fighting or flight. Remember that the fight or flight reaction is always meant to end in a vigorous physical activity–fighting or fleeing away from danger. Running up and downstairs, sitting up, running quickly or walking fast, something sweating is enough to bring fighting or flight to its natural conclusion. But training also has a calming role. This is not always necessary. There has been plenty of studies that make people less nervous, depressed, and lonely five minutes a week jumper-even if they are not during an anxiety attack. This needs five minutes, that's everything. If you are not hot or sweaty, it is just as good to walk briskly for 20-30 minutes five times a week. The benefit of practice on mental health is defined. (In fact, it's that good, has the same impact on health as antidepressants.) It was the topic of extensive study and has shown that it is always valid.

2. Learn what symptoms you don't have.

You don't have a heart attack, you remember. Heart injuries would probably occur when the middle of the thorn becomes lacking movement, discomfort or pain and jaw pain, pain in either armor in both, usually in the left side of the upper body.

You don't go crazy, you know. The very idea that you can wonder if you're nuts or not implies, you're not. Those who are unable to question or to worry about their state of mind are lacking in knowledge and insight.

3. Don't fight it.

Anxiety feeds you until afterwards, you're afraid of anxiety. The more you fight, the more it becomes. He thinks it's there, remembers, to protect you. The more you embrace your fear and make sure it takes care of you, the sooner the distress disappears.

Remember if your anxiety is an over-vigilant brain physical, neurological response. Remember to mention the respiratory techniques that will alleviate your physical symptoms.

4. Mindfulness.

When the word itself invokes the aroma of incense and lenses and the perspective of Skye Liberty Rain as a dreamcatcher and friends of astral life, then you have to know: Harvard Medical School is on board to describe awareness as a powerful therapeutic tool. The way it works is through better brain interactions. Research has also shown that depression & anxiety can be reduced, sleep, mood & memory enhanced, learning encourages, the breathing improves, heart activity improves, and immunity improves. Just be conscious will clear your mind, slow down fear, slow down your nervous system, improve focus and relax. Within Buddhism, the concept of mindfulness has its origins. This is a helpful way of triggering a calming reaction which involves looking or watching, without judging, what is happening today. Briefly, it is the other way around.

5. Now the how: Centre.

Shut your eyes and feel your body. Concentrate on breathing. How does the air look like having it within you? Note air sensation, when rising up and fall on your abdomen. Notice the beating of your heart.

Wide. Once your concentration is reduced to what you feel inside, begin expanding your focus. What could you hear? Feeling? What are your ideas? Taking each without assessing or examining. If your mind begins wandering, concentrate on your breathing again.

Watch. Watch what crosses your mind as well as what makes you feel happy and find out what emotions are leading to your suffering. Try not to focus on an idea, feeling or sensation. Similarly, try not to think about both the past or the future.

Stay with that. Try to implement a few times a week 20 to 40 minutes of attention. Start slowly and gradually if that sounds like a lot. Mindfulness can be as straightforward as trying to listen to what is going on around you–listening to the music, moving about it, but really concentrating on it. It's worth the results.

To try to "solve" the problem that causes it, it is common for anxiety to try frenziedly for the factors behind all the symptoms. Since fear is often wrongly caused, without any real problem, it is fruitless to try and identify the source, yet the fear persists.

6. Switch it off.

The idea is to give the mind a rest from stress about the same stuff over and over, or nothing. Sit down and close your eyes silently. Assume a box that is open and ready for all your worries. See, name and put every problem in the box. If you don't have issues, shut the package and visualize putting it somewhere, perhaps a shelf or a closet or under the pillow, until you have to come back for something. Once you have removed the box, let the remaining space in your mind occupy itself with what is the most relevant feeling and thought for you.

7. Alright, worry, but just once.

Maybe the only path is clear via the middle. Worrying about something so that you pay full exposure can help to stop it from playing in your mind over and over. Grant yourself a 10-20minute time limit and worry about all of the problems that bother you. Set the time again to worry. While they are coming up again, note that you have cared about them and scheduled time for them to return. Divide your focus and emotions to a different activity easily. A ready list of potential diversions could be useful.

Chapter 5: A healthy mind and a better life

The peace of mind in a world in which there is plenty of stress, burden, rush and unrest, is of great importance. It is a privilege that everybody needs, but very few will achieve it, or even fewer will do it. This is a state of inner calm, peace and relaxation that produces gladness, patience, inner consistency and self-control. Mental peace is a learned skill which, like every other ability, takes time, practice as well as perseverance. You will at least reach a degree of inner peace with the right training even with desire, determination, patience and perseverance. There's nothing better than peace. Inner peace really does not entirely guide or eradicate our fears and anxieties, but inner happiness allows us to cope with fear and anxiety and aspire to go beyond that. Many people have trillions of dollars on their list but have no peacefulness. There are many benefits to inner comfort. If you're good, you're clearly thinking, innovating and planning. If you are calm, it won't really influence you what people think of you. You are not affected by events and sometimes, challenges. This allows us to focus more on the work we have to do. We are efficient in our everyday business. It enables us to build a sense of patience, knowledge, inner strength, inner happiness and satisfaction.

5.1 Why Peace of mind is important?

Peace of mind is not always found by monks and hermits on the Himalayas. It is achievable here and, wherever you are, regardless of your external circumstances, as it is an internal state, independent of external circumstances and conditions. Peace is revealed when the mind slows down constant inner chat. Anxiety, pain, depression, terror, emotional and mental distress, nervousness and frustration are eliminated as they arise. Peace of mind allows you to show calmness and peace in your everyday life as well as in challenging and difficult situations. This allows you to show mental and emotional isolation when possible, and therefore to prevent the phrases, thoughts and actions of others being too influenced. You can also regulate your emotions and become an open-minded, peaceful, compassionate, tolerant person. There are different techniques to calm your mind, and even just a few minutes a day, you will follow and implement these techniques and soon become conscious of constructive inner improvements within yourself.

You won't have to wait until you could start working on the perfect circumstances. You should continue here and now, no matter what life you lead and no matter what your conditions are. This may take some effort, but it's a worthwhile project, with great rewards. You should live your own life, maintain your careers and marriages, and still work to achieve inner peace, without altering their outward situation. This is done gradually by trying to change your mind, through cultivating inner strength and isolation, through reflection and other methods.

Importance of Peace of mind

Internal peace does not only apply to those who devote their lives to prayer or religion. Inner harmony can be reached, regardless of the way we live or work. As told earlier, inner prosperity can be discovered as we learn to see the world around us attentively. Inner peace, without distracting emotions, is a state of mental and emotional health which acknowledges our regulation over moods and reactions. To inner peace, it is important that we accept that this is true and that we feel our reasoning, feelings and actions are regulated. When we genuinely believe and accept that, we have formed the foundations of inner peace.

When you reach inner peace, you find that you can handle every event or situation around you in a healthy way. Inner peace doesn't really drive our anxieties and fears completely or eradicate them, but internal harmony helps us to deal with the anxieties and fears and strive to go beyond. No anxieties or fears can be eliminated but fears and anxieties can be used as a means of further growth.

There are just a few explanations for the importance of inner peace.

1. It enhances our ability to concentrate. There are several challenges in today's world that trigger our anxiety as well as worry. We don't have the anxiety and worry that make us lose concentration at ourselves and our households. Inner peace shows us the best way to cope so that we can transform our fear, stress and intervention while maintaining our eyes centered on what really counts in our lives.

2. This allows us to show endurance and perseverance. If you have any experience with social media, you realize that these days there seems to be a lack of patience and awareness. With internal peace, we can be compassionate and respectful of other people's views without the need for vengeance or responses. Through wisdom, we can better understand know the situation and thus better understand the solutions to the problems. Inner peace tells one

3. It gives us a better sleeping ability. Either for we are overstressed, or our minds overworked, many of us don't get the right amount of sleep. Since internal harmony helps us interact with our worries and problems, it not only allows us to focus but also makes us slow down so that we can sleep well at night.

4. It allows us to have joy. Happiness is but a feeling that passes away, though an emotion that isn't simple in these days. With a feeling of inner peace and thus less anxiety and stress, we will feel happier times more profoundly. If we live consciously and have a feeling of inner peace, the joy times feel bigger but seem to linger forever.

5. Our relations with others are improved. How we think regarding ourselves is how the world around us perceives us. Our reactions and behaviors are driven by this perspective. Once I have inner peace, I will change my own perspective, so the environment around me will be better and brighter, contributing to more positive responses and behavior on my side. The more confident I may be in my interactions, the more optimistic I will be.

6. Liberation in Emotion. It lets you handle your response to events around you more efficiently. Traumatic events or people who treat you unfairly may include this. You will try a peaceful place to analyze what takes place and how you cope with it by allowing yourself independence from emotional reactions.

7. Liberty from pessimistic thoughts. You can control your thoughts as though the brain is a muscle that you can work out? According to several various sources, the reaction is "yes." You should monitor the emotions and function through a concentration in the discipline in order to get rid of intrusive feelings concerning unpleasant issues. This is supported by science. Several studies have demonstrated that change of mind will affect how the environment around you perceives. An optimistic mindset will contribute to a calmer existence. Yourselves, though, will strive to "transform your reality." You have to consider the way you speak and dismiss critical concerns.

8. Liberty from the Judgment of Others. It is essential to everyone what people assume of us. That's a good thing to some degree. We want to behave in such a way that others are glad to be there. Though we are often too concerned about other people's opinions. This can direct us to act in ways we would never behave otherwise. It can be truly liberating to be able to free yourself from this type of concern.

9. From the Inner Critique, Release Yourself. It goes hand-in-hand with the freedom from bad thinking. But all of them are self-created in this case. There is a message we have been told somewhere along the path that certain things should be completed, and we struggle if we do not do so. We grow nagging thoughts and feelings, which we constantly criticize. It is important to know that everything is in our own minds! Not everyone can be rid of all those inner voices and "escape." It doesn't have to be flawless at all times in our existence. Relax and to be ourselves is necessary. Peace is a subject that many consider, not always. Take the time and energy you need to recognize forms in which you are not safe. Focusing on freedom can bring peace, harmony and productivity to a much more calm life.

5.2 Seven laws of peace of mind

Peace of mind is a condition of peace and harmony with your thoughts, mentally and spiritually. You need ample understanding and knowledge to relax in the face of conflict and tension. How wonderful it would be to be quiet, focused and anxious!! We can choose to remain emotionally, mentally, and unwavering, rather than having anxious and fearful.

7 Laws of Peace of Mind

Nothing is better than peace. Even no achievement. There are a lot of people on their list who have billions of dollars but have no peace of mind. If you are cool, you will clearly think, formulate creative ideas and execute your plans. It just represents the behavior when you are depressed all the time. Below are the seven laws of peace that will allow you to regain your life balance.

1. You cannot travel across life with a foot in the past. What you do in your past is important to make peace with. Do whatever it takes to find a solution if it is troubling you. If for something which happened previously, you feel guilty, sadness, sorrow or anger, learn the lessons and pass on. If you've done anything wrong, make changes. Speak to a trusted person or call for professional help if you are lost. You will feel well in the past and tell you important life lessons about the experience you have created. Find a peaceful spirit in your past.

2. Stop caring about what others think because people are too worried about their actions; often don't take risks in their career. These people never avoided a boring job as a guitarist or an artist. We have to appear good and sell their aspirations before their mates. But they don't know that even doing what they enjoy they will excel. Stop your life in search of others ' approval. You can be your best judge, and nothing is cooler than your own heart's speech. Having a peaceful mind, follow your heart.

3. Time Heals, sometimes all we have to do sometimes is to slacken and allow time to heal our wounds. Of course, with your healing time from inside, it's also what you say.

Because you are able to drown in alcohol or follow another auto destructive path to deal with pain, or you can realize the pain as well as take positive measures to treat pain in a healthy manner, such as exercise, yoga or therapy. Take time to heal your wounds and give you a quiet mind.

4. "Happiness is what you believe, speak and do in love," states Gandhi–Mahatma. Only once you assume full responsibility for life should you make any changes. You and Nobody else is liable for your happiness. Those who blame others for their shortcomings or external circumstances are not only wrong but also give away their power. The answer is to be accountable and to build your life as you want. If you want more money, build skills; if you want a relationship, get together with people with the same mind. For a fact, what you focus on is always a pleasure. Concentrate on the good, and you will be happy, concentrate on the bad, and you will be miserable. Take control of your mind, focus your attention, and you will feel calm.

5. Do not compare yourself to others because your trip is totally distinct. Whether in terms of monetary success, looks or anything, when we compare ourselves with others, we do unfairness to ourselves. Everyone is on a path of its own. See how far you have come and respect your contributions. We often overlook how solid we are when we feel depressed. It is essential to honor your journey and not concentrate on others to be calm.

6. Stop thinking over. It's all right not to know the answers. It's all right not to ask anything. Yes, the world's most successful individuals don't all learn. You just act to find answers along the way. And so, they maintain a calm, thoughtless mind. Everyone can figure out life along the way, regardless as successful or popular. Living is like running. You can't be too scared or go on the boat. And without taking the risk, you cannot know how to run.

7. Smile. All the problems of the world you do not have to fix are the best blessings in the world. Take on your face always with a smile, not because life is simple, but because it's worth it.

5.3 How to find peace of mind and happiness?

Why would you think it is important to keep calm?

The inner peace of mind provides many advantages. If you have peace of mind, what people believe about you will not really influence you. Events or challenges do not affect you. This enables us to focus better on the job we are tasked with. We are making our day-to-day affairs more efficient. It allows us to develop a sense of patience and understanding, inner strength, inner pleasure, and satisfaction.

How could we bring inner peace?

Eventually, inner peace can contribute to outside stability. You take it into your external and other people's lives, by building peace into your inner world, in your mind. Here are some of the signs to achieve a calm and peaceful state:

1. ACCEPTANCE: Acceptance is the key element for peace of mind. We have to recognize, and we have to agree that life is really all about uncertainty. Whatever you can and can't control, we must differentiate. Acceptance also applies to your faith and knowledge of your emotional needs.

2. DE-CLUTTER: Feelings can make emotional distress more stressful. We have to learn the feelings to find effective methods to have clear outs on a regular basis.

3. MINDFULNESS: We are fully present and conscious with our five senses when we are alive. This gives us less time to worry about the other stressors and to think about them.

4. SELF LOVE: The further we accept and love each other, the greater our peace of mind is reached. We will live with any tough situation until we embrace ourselves.

5. BE TRUE WITH YOUR SELF: It's another key element for soothing our souls. They are similar to the way they think and feel as we exercise kindness. We must be careful of our emotions and thoughts as it affects the tests.

How to choose peacefulness and happiness

You must learn how to use the key in order to achieve happiness and peace of mind. It improves your health and your arousal. Read on to understand how to choose peacefulness and happiness.

1. Listen to music.

Studies show that children with ADHD can be calmer and more concentrated by relaxing music. But what kind of music you choose to listen to doesn't matter, as long as you enjoy and relax? Music is the nourishment for the soul, an immediate way to calm down.

2. Breathing exercises.

If you concentrate on your breathing, the mind is concentrated on the cycle of air and exhalation that enhances your life. Make it five long, powerful blows and concentrate on your palm and diaphragm. This is a fast and easiest way to feel calm instantly.

3. Just go into a Walk.

Entering the fresh air will make yourself a nice world and foster peace of mind. Take a break and pump blood–particularly when the sun shines.

4. Feel and Enjoy Nature.

Too much concreteness is never an excellent thing. You can actually feel younger and happier by investing time in nature. That's why. Please leave the city for a period. Hear the singing of birds and enjoy tranquility and peace.

5. Play with Pets.

Having a pet is an excellent way to relieve stress. Touch is a strong sensation that can relieve tension and foster peace of mind.

6. Declutter.

Have clear outs regularly. Clutter will increase stress, and a better and more relaxed environment is possible in a tidy, orderly house.

7. Agreement.

For comfort, acceptance is necessary. It is a huge leap in stakes of peace of mind that we accept that the world has few guarantees and learn to tolerate uncertainty. Distinguish what you can and can't control.

8. Attention.

We are fully present, fully aware of our five senses, when we are mindful: touch, taste, sight, listening and smell. Commit your senses. This gives your mind less time to worry about "what ifs."

9. Love for yourself.

The more we love ourselves, the more tranquil our mind is. Whatever the situation we find ourselves in, we embrace ourselves further and feel at ease in the world. Our inner harmony is strengthened, and we feel less uncertainty.

10. Be truthful to you.

It's another vital part of mental harmony. We have similarly as we feel and think when we exercise congruence. We practice conformity when we see ourselves as well as the way life sees us. Problems arise if we look one way (as a loving mother, for example), but we do not see each other (e.g., neglect our kids because we're too busy, for example). One of the secrets to peace of mind is to find ways to maintain our inner ideals and similar behavior.

11. Humor.

Laugh very much. If you see the hilarious side of life, the world is immediately a better place. Laughter is a great stress reliever and releases hormones to help us relax.

12. Unconditional love.

This makes it much easier to love beyond fear if you do not foresee something. Our unfulfilled expectations can generate inner turmoil as well as feelings of resentment if we love the conditions. Insecurity kills calmness.

13. Go to Health Checks regularly.

It's worth checking and taking care of your health. Letting oneself go may show a lack of respect for one's self, and that in turn, affects how we see the world and how others communicate with us. Be friendly to yourself and do your best.

14. Take Stock.

From time to time, checking if you're satisfied with the quality of your life is a good idea. Are you interested in your job? Your association? Are you on the right path? Make changes to restoring peace of mind if possible.

15. Have objectives.

This connects with the 14th. The goals keep us on the right path and give us meaning. Design your goals SMART.

16. Not to Take Yourself seriously.

This concerns No. 11. Learn to make your approach to life more flexible. The tougher our opinions are, the better the circumstances can be met that clash with our static ideas.

17. Live at the moment.

Rather than worry about the past or fear for the future, enjoy the NOW. This particular moment, it's all we got. The problems of the past and the future cannot be concerned when we live in the moment.

18. Worry less.

We seem to have between 30,000-75,000 thoughts a day, 80% of whom are spontaneous "nonsense." Learn to think about shelving by realizing that most of your problems have been unproductive, eliminating any possibility of peace of mind.

19. Be stubborn.

You have the right to be here as much as anyone else and to get an opinion. We do not serve ourselves if we become passive and perhaps submissive.

Being confident is not about your (aggressive) need or your (passive) need ahead of others. It's more about compromise— a situation of "win-win."

21. Voice your opinion.

 Don't be scared to say what you have in mind. This is in keeping with being self-confident. Ask what in life you want. Don't you get it, if you don't ask?

22. Explore "Me-Time."

It is important to time out. A little egotistic time to support yourself or do just as you like to meet the unreasonable demands of life. Equilibrium is essential in life.

23. Frolic.

The free web vocabulary defines the word "frolic" as: "to act with a playful and uninhibited eye. Take the time to enjoy things. Try to make fun of cases that aren't especially pleasant. Adjust life to a funny attitude. When did you let the child in you play last?

24. Just let go.

You simply can't change those things regardless of how hard you strive. Know when and how to cut your losses and detach (as Elsa does!) 24. Defeat Guilt.

Guilt is indeed a negative emotion which destroys tranquility. Although (in the wrong way) it can inspire us, it remains a toxic emotion. Challenge the motives for your guilt to ensure that you do not pressure yourself unnecessarily.

25. Start taking a mindset of gratitude.

Concentrating on all things we're grateful for in our lives fosters peace of mind and keeps reminding us that it is always good. We have to shift our consciousness occasionally.

26. See the Learning Curve for failure.

Failure really does have bad connotations, but everyone fails. Could you get anything better or know if you don't fail? A positive attitude to failure promotes bravery. You're not the one. Instead, it's what you wanted to do. The difference is enormous.

27. Talk with others.

One of life's real joys is to share lives with others and to know that others "get" you. We feel a little less alone; understanding gives us a fantastic sense of comfort.

28. Check your limits.

When you always stay in your comfort zone, you will never come to know your true potential. It's better than regretting all those things that you wanted you tried, as the saying says, and regret what you have done. Learn to leave your area of comfort.

29. Search for Positive Emotion Outlets.

Games, online forums, visitors of the same mind, hobbies anything that takes your fancy. Avoiding negative feelings can cause health problems. Drop social stress and anger and feel much happier.

30. Slow it down.

Why does it all have to be done today? Even when we don't have to, we put unnecessary pressure upon ourselves. Keep challenging your impatience, be conscious and experience life right now.

31. Test "Shoulds" and "Maybes."

Self-induced stress never leads to peace of mind or inner calmness. Substitute "must" with "must" and live more of life in your own terms.

32. Be Kind.

It is free and makes a change. It also gives us all an inner boost if we show kindness.

33. Don't compare.

The more we make comparisons, the more we get lost. Forget what all others do or say. What do you want? There are all our own paths, and we all learn and work in our own rhythm. Concentrate on your every journey as well as lose the pressure of comparing with what you think happens in other people's lives. This is a safe way for peace of mind to be exercised.

34. The statements.

Talk positively to yourself with claims. One good example of a person encouraging peace of mind is: "I'll find a way to get through it, no matter what's going on in my way." Believe in yourself and regularly remember you will be all right.

35. As much as you can, save some money.

It's a good idea to put money aside. Do it regularly if you can save money. You're not even going to realize it is gone, start a daily debit every month.

36. Less is More.

Money buys many choices and options, but not the joy we want. Be content with those of the simplest things in life–from here comes true joy and tranquility.

37. The outlook.

Take a look at the bigger picture always. Will you feel like this next week, or in a year? Is your current life experience as important? You're going to be fine more often than not. Encourage peace of mind through the maintenance of life perspective.

38. Control your thoughts.

The quality of our life could be made or destroyed by our feelings. Make sure you choose to speak for yourself. As a best friend, speak to yourself. Self-loathing is futile and will surely bring happiness out of your life.

39. Rise up for what you know.

Whether it protects animals or helps the less fortunate ones, follow your heart and passion. Combat the desire to fit in and see what you expect. You donate your peace of mind when you change to fit others.

40. Have enough sleep.

Hardly anything goes smoothly when we are tired and grumpy. Get eight hours of sleep a night and get your body regenerated.

The most effective ways for soothing yourself are to be faithful to yourself, to acknowledge that life is unpredictable and to look at your thoughts. Many of us "torture" us mentally daily with our own things.

5.4 Some tips and advice

Life could be stressful — juggling with family, friends, career and the daily burden of payment and sales. Don't get overwhelmed! Therapy and medicines are what you don't have to turn. Attempt these ten easy habits which can help you survive without anxiety, instead of allowing life to give you a panique.

1. Boring routines creation.

You don't have to concern about an unidentified variable that throws your whole day out if you do the same thing day by day. Your commute to work every morning and every afternoon you head home the same way. Perform a daily routine that means you do everything without having to take time. Next, check your email, focus on your energy works and projects right after lunch. Understanding what happens in your day reduces the uncertain anxiety

2. Write down your thoughts.

Maintain a journal. It might sound young or long-term, but it helps! Writing down your ideas will take you out of your head; if you already have them written, you may feel more relaxed, but you do not have to think so often. Seeing them on writing could also help you work more clearly than if you run around.

3. Research your anxiety.

Stop thinking about what makes you feel this way and why when you are anxious. Knowing what will allow you to control your fear and maybe work out how to avoid it in the future! You will always be concerned about an extension to launch the job early if you have busy working time. Once you learn the root, there are ways to fight and manage your fear.

4. Accept the inconvenience.

Accept it when you begin to be worried! Nobody likes to feel uncomfortable, but you can help to control your anxiety if you stop feeling frustrated. The pain of an anxiety attack is often so intense that it induces growing fear which unnecessarily prolongs the crisis. Consider the feelings to see how they allow you to manage your fear.

5. Regular exercise.

Physical exercise helps greatly combat fear and depressive emotions. Enable your ideas to control your emotions, act instead of running around the room! Visit the fitness center to conduct a workout. Travel around the city. Pushups, lift weights, make stretches. If you keep your body active, it keeps your mind busy and wears you out as an extra bonus, so that you can easily fall asleep without throwing and transforming while your brain is taken over by anxious thoughts.

6. Take your time to relax.

It makes it sound like the other way round, right? Work hard. Play hard! One way you can conquer fear is to continue to cram your day so full. Don't be scared to say no to other people or events to keep time. Relax totally when you relax. Don't look at Television or keep the phone connected. Allow your mind to go blank; let your bodies go limp to see how cool you feel when you stand up.

7. Divert yourself.

The imagination is too strong to think and stress about the worst in any case before it occurs. When you start feeling anxious, your brain ties on and will not let go before you have a full-blown attack. You must monitor your own minds and inhibit. Perform logical problems, arithmetic concerns or reverse the letter. These seem straightforward ideas, but the issues are complicated enough for the brain to digest and cause all your worries to float away.

8. Stop drinking caffeine.

I mean, it's complicated! Hopefully, it could be enough to try to stop drinking caffeine, as suggested by the last tip! Caffeine, though, is a stimulant, and you will not be allowed to sleep in large amounts. Caffeine is proven to boost your alertness, focus and memory, but you do not have the ability to concentrate and jitter if you are already nervous, then these positive factors can quickly turn into a moving back. Cutting caffeine means that you cut something that will most probably help to cause anxiety attacks.

9. Encourage good thinking.

Although it seems impossible to feel depressed, make yourself believe positive! Anxiety cannot last indefinitely, and before long tension must fade. Transform yourself into something good in every scenario that disturbs you.

Tell yourself, your fear will pass until you know. Your anxiety is groundless.

10. Have a group of friends.

This does not mean that you must participate in group therapy–it simply means that you have a group that you can talk with and trust. It is important, to be honest with each other, so ensure that your network is crowded with people whom you trust. Once you express your thoughts, you will feel better, and you will receive better input and advice.

Tips for creating happiness and peace in life

1) The possessions and conditions are not entitled to peace and happiness. Material goods, money and fame, can bring temporary gladness and inner peace, but you can bring true happiness and peace. You are not contingent on your own land, rank or circumstances. Satisfaction and happiness are also the stuff you enjoy, like playing a good game, having friends, driving, or a hobby. When you do little, practical things that you love, you will experience several periods of peace daily.

2) Take a positive life outlook. Speak about ideas, not of challenges. You can choose between seeing the problems and seeing the remedies. You can predict disappointment and expect success. You may choose success. Forget about the past and reflect on the moment. You feel light, relaxed and calm through a positive attitude.

3) Don't you let the anxiety take care of your thoughts? Can't you terrified or lose your job? Are you concerned you don't have enough money to pay the rent? Are you concerned about someone you love not gaining the heart of? Fear and anxiety tend to tension and dissatisfaction. Even though your fears and concerns are true, you won't get anything, except for lack of happiness and peace.

Don't let your ego control negative thinking. What you might not know, and if it does, you will not do any good by thinking about it. You can only benefit from positive thoughts as well as a positive action.

4) Be an advisor. Don't actually accept the facts. Don't be passive. Be involved, be an activist. Don't be afraid of the challenges and action. You always want to have it, but you have no time or money? Would you like something to do, but do you not have the confidence to do it?

It's time for a change now. If you do what you love, you will be filled with happiness and peace.

5) Modify what you don't like and decide to change things that don't or that don't benefit you Consciously. Maybe you can't change anything, yet in your life, you can change many things.

Would you like to visit a particular country? Would you like to move to a new apartment or house? Ever feel stuck in a position and would like you to be able to change it? Are your marriages having problems?

Consider such improvements as initiatives that will improve your life. Taking an idea, dream about it, prepare and begin to work on it. You will be satisfied and happier as you make the change you desire.

6) Give your time to your family. Find your energy, chat, play and have fun with your kids. Have dinner with them, at least once per week. Make time to spend a vacation or trip.